SQL Server with C#

Klaus Elk

ISBN-13: 978-1720358671
ISBN-10: 1720358672

See also https://klauselk.com

Preface

In-between working with embedded systems, I have worked with PC-software. Sometimes the applications were "real" products - sometimes internal tools. Many applications had databases within them, and I learned as I went along.

I have tried various frameworks and tools, "strange" languages like Modula-2, and object-oriented databases, but it wasn't until my most recent project that it felt really good. So what went right?

I decided to write this book - to revisit the theory and code, to learn, and hopefully to pass on some know-how. I have written about all the subjects that became relevant in relation to the project - during design, implementation and maintenance.

Einstein said: *"Make it as simple as possible, but not simpler"*. You will see that I generally aim for simple solutions and simple tools. There's a beauty in not throwing every tool and every pattern in the book into a solution.

The first part of the book introduces general database theory and SQL - with SQL Server as the specific example. The second part is about the related C# programming. ADO.net is used here "as is" without frameworks on top - being a time-proven framework by itself. The two parts of the book are bridged through a common sample - the project that "went right".

Full source can be downloaded - see links on https://klauselk.com.

About The Author

Klaus Elk is a Master of Science in Electronics from the Danish Technical University of Copenhagen, with a thesis on digital signal processing. He also holds a Bachelor's degree in Marketing. For many years he has worked in the industry within the domains of telecommunication, medical electronics and sound and vibration. He has worked mainly with embedded systems, but also with PC software.

In a period of 10 years Klaus Elk - besides his R&D job - taught at the Danish Technical University. The subjects were object-oriented programming (C++ and Java), and the Internet Protocol Stack. Today he is R&D Manager in Instrumentation at HBK - the former Brüel & Kjær Sound & Vibration. Klaus is also the author of "Embedded Software for the IoT" - of which the 3'rd edition recently was published by De Gruyter.

Acknowledgements

A big "Thank You" goes to my colleagues. They were the first subjected to the sample in this book: a time-registration system. Such a system is never popular among developers, but they took it standing. In this book I describe how the system was created in a way that bothered the developers as little as possible, while giving the best possible data to management. It even enabled project-managers to explain why their projects was sometimes lagging behind.

I also want to thank my manager - Lars Agerlin - for letting me publish the sample code.

Klaus Elk

Contents

Chapter 1

Introduction

1.1   What to expect from this book

If you are planning to write a database-application and have little or no experience beforehand, there are a many questions:

- ❐ What is an RDBMS - and how does it differ from a database?

- ❐ How do you pick the right one - and where does SQL Server fit in?

- ❐ They say SQL Server is of the OLTP type. What does that mean - and what is the alternative?

- ❐ How do I create a database and its tables - and especially the relations and constraints?

- ❐ Understanding the above - how do I do it in a "good" design?

- ❐ What about the application? How is it layered?

- ❐ Where does ADO.net fit into all this?

- ❐ What about all the small tricks that makes it all work in the end?

- ❐ How do I get data into Excel - preferably without additional libraries?

- ❐ Show me the code!

1

Hopefully you will find that these questions, as well as many others, are answered. There are many tools that will get you to a certain point, but without a deeper understanding you begin to go in circles, making modifications based on questionable assumptions. The aim of this book is to provide this understanding. There are no exercises, however it is possible to "code along", using official Microsoft tools - see Section 1.2.

To help clarify the text, typesetting is as follows:

- ❏ Itemized lists are like this, while sequential lists are numbered - starting with: ①

- ❏ PascalCase is used for tables, columns etc. in the database.

- ❏ camelCase is used for C# variables and functions.

- ❏ *Italic* for keywords, the first time they occur locally. *Italics* are also used for standard classes and library functions - e.g. *DataGridView*, while code in the sample is introduced first using quotes - like "MyFlag".

- ❏ SMALL CAPS is used for emphasized statements.

- ❏ Plain tables are used for database tables and other computed output. A plain table has vertical as well as horizontal single-width separating lines all over. Contrary to this, authored tables do not have any vertical lines, while they use bold headers and other formatting.

- ❏ Standard captions. Meaning that captions are under figures, but above listings and tables.

- ❏ Chapters, sections and subsections are numbered.

- ❏ Code in boxes and inline like:
  ```
  SELECT ProjectID FROM Projects WHERE Name = 'Vacation'
  ```

- ❏ SQL code is formatted "compact" to save space. Check out some of the many free on-line formatters.

1.2 Tools

All code in the sample as well as all code-snippets and concepts described in this book can be created with the help of two Microsoft Tools:

❐ **Microsoft Visual Studio Community Edition**
Microsoft Visual Studio is by far the most advanced IDE (integrated development environment) found today. Microsoft has a good position in the corporate world, but also aims to become more relevant to the "grassroots" and the open source community. Years ago Microsoft handed over the C# language to an independent organ, and now we have the *Community Edition* of Visual Studio - free to use for any single developer as well as certain minor organizations.

The Community Edition is surprisingly powerful, and we really don't need more for this book. It even runs on Mac OSX. The only programming language used in this book is C# - if not considering SQL a programming language. With Visual Studio comes not only the C# compiler and debugger, but also all the class libraries needed. Some of the most relevant for databases are *ADO.net* and *linq*.

❐ **Microsoft SQL Management Studio with SQL Server Express**
As stated above, Microsoft has the corporate presence, but also to a degree reaches out to the open source developers. SQL Server now runs on some *Linux* distributions. It even - optionally - runs on *Docker*. This is a *Container* on Linux - which is kind of a lightweight *Virtual Machine* without a guest/host OS.

SQL Server comes in many editions - from the *Enterprise Edition*, over the *Standard Edition* to the *LocalDB*. There is also a *Developer Edition* which essentially is the same as the Enterprise Edition. The Standard and Enterprise SQL Servers are not free, but you can get very far with the free Express edition.

I have not found any functionality in the big SQL Servers that I really miss in the Express edition. The main difference is scale: The Express edition "only" supports up to 10 GB databases and only utilizes a single CPU[1]. This makes it a great choice for development: it is

---

[1]At the time of this writing: Max 4 cores, max 1410 MB pool buffer size and max 352 MB Column-store segment cache.

ready to port to SQL Server. It actually also makes it an interesting candidate for minor real installations.

LocalDB deviates from the others by not being run as a separate service. Instead, it can be run directly as a part of an application. Many users may run each their instance of this on the same PC. This makes it behave more like a powerful version of *MS Access*.

Finally, *Azure SQL* is modeled very closely to SQL Server, and what you learn in this book can also be applied to Azure SQL.

With the installation we get not just the server, but also the IDE for SQL-development with the handy name *Microsoft SQL Server Management Studio*. Even abbreviated to *MSSMS* this name is hard to remember. The good thing is that once installed, you can just type "SQL" after pressing the Windows Home button to find it. In this book we will use the shorter form "Management Studio".

A third tool - not from Microsoft, but highly recommended - is *git*. This book is not about source-control. However, you should not work with code without a source-control system. This is where C#-code and database-scripts are stored and version-managed. Surely, any version-control system will do, but these days "git is it".

As a single developer you can download and use all the above tools for free.

1.3   TimeReg Sample

Through the book we will use an existing application as a sample - binding together database theory, SQL and C# code. The sample is a time-registration system called TimeReg.

The TimeReg sample is used extensively in the C# part of this book. It is a good example because it uses terms that most developers are familiar with, and thus do not require extra domain knowledge. We can focus on the actual database subjects.

Generally only managers like Time-Registration. This might be to control the employees, but in reality it is more likely that it controls the quality of

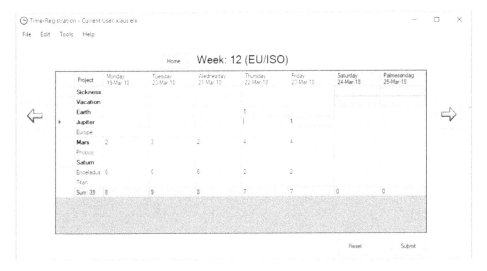

Figure 1.1: Resulting Main Screen

the management. A manager may say one day that project A has the highest priority, and then the next day that project B has the highest priority. With a Time-Registration system the truth will out. Here you see which task or project got priority in the end. Thus, it may also be a good tool for a project manager or developer as he can say: "We did not put the planned effort into this project, because we had to spend a lot of time on task X". If you calculate *velocity* in a project, time-registration is also a help. Thus, in some ways the burden of e.g. not meeting targets is now shared with the management - as it should be. The good thing is that it also indicates to management what they need to do: less of this and more of that.

Figure 1.1 shows the main screen in the implemented sample program. It looks very simple, and indeed it is - as long as you only need to input hours. The screen shown on the figure is what all users experience when they need to type in hours. This main workflow is the one we look closest into, but there are in fact a number of other screens and workflows. We will examine some of these, but far from all.

If you want to download the sample database and/or the C#-code, please go to https://klauselk.com to learn how.

Part I

SQL Server

Chapter 2

Database Basics

2.1 Database Vocabulary

There are several very different types of databases. Twenty years ago I experimented with an *bject-oriented database* called *POET*. This concept seemed like a good idea - after all, when we work with objects, it is practical to store and retrieve them directly to/from the database without any tedious mapping. However, there was still the need for a mapping, as the database only supported its own basic data-types, and only its own collections. On top of this, it was not possible to analyze the data with 3'rd-party tools. Maybe these are the reasons that we don't hear much about object-oriented databases today.

In this book we are dealing with *relational databases* - which means table-based databases. There are many ways to construct a relational database. Vendors give their implementation a more or less standardized external interface - allowing us to use SQL - *Structured Query Language*. The entire system - low-level implementation of tables etc. with SQL-interface - is known as an *RDBMS - Relational Database Management System*. Specifically in this book we are dealing almost exclusively with *Microsoft SQL Server*.

As is often the case, the interface (SQL) is not completely standardized - vendors need some space for marketing their particular version. Still, almost everything written in this book also holds true for other RDBMSs like Oracle and MySQL/MariaDB, although sometimes the syntax deviates a little. In this book I follow the usual terms - using "RDBMS" for the product that you get from e.g. Microsoft, and "database" for the thing you create in it.

You probably already have an idea of what the main terms in databases mean. There are, however, many misunderstandings and words with multiple meanings. It is difficult to describe some terms without using the others. For this reason I will briefly introduce the most important parts of the SQL Server hierarchy in Table 2.1. This continues in Table 2.2 with the most important database concepts. We will meet them all again.

The discussion on *records* & *fields* versus *rows* & *columns* can be a pain. Early PC-databases used a mixture of the terms. "records" and "fields" are often used in UI-software, and "records" are also used at the file-level in databases. In Excel, we use "rows" and "columns". No wonder most of us use "row" and "record" for the same thing, and the same goes for "column" and "field". However, the standards and even Microsoft says:

A DATABASE-TABLE CONSISTS OF ROWS AND COLUMNS.

Thus, we will use "row" and "column" in this book. The term "Field" is also sometimes used for a specific column and row intersection. Naturally this will be referred to as a *Cell*.

Table 2.1: The SQL Server hierarchy

Name	Meaning
RDBMS	Relational database management system - a table-based system with SQL-interface.
Server	This can mean the hardware or the SQL Server that runs on it. In this book it is the latter.
Database	In daily speak the database is often the same as the server. More correctly, a single database-server hosts one or more databases. In Connection Strings you refer to a *catalog*.
Schema	Used for grouping tables inside a database - like a namespace in C#. It brings the additional ability to have different security schemes inside the same database. Generally you can get very far with the default *dbo* schema.
Table	This is the basic entity of a relational database. It is always 2-dimensional. The full-name of a table on a given server is $< database > . < schema > . < table >$
View	A construction within the database that in many ways looks as a table to the clients.
Row	This is a row in a table. In an Employees table, one row is one employee. Sometimes called a "record".
Column	This is a column in a table. In an Employees table it might be the salary number. Sometimes called a "field".
Cell	A specific cell in a table. Sometimes called a "field".

Table 2.2: Important database concepts

Name	Meaning
OLTP	On-line transaction processing. As opposed to OLAP.
OLAP	On-line analytical processing.
CRUD	Create, retrieve, update and delete are the main functions of a database.
ACID	Atomicity, consistency, isolation & durability. Main features of a good RDBMS.
Primary Key	One or more columns that together defines a unique row in the given table
Foreign Key	One or more columns that together points to a unique row in (typically) another table
Normal Form	This is a categorization of how correct the database is structured. From non-normalized we step through 1'st Normal Form - 1NF - over 2NF, 3NF, 4NF and 5NF. Usually we don't go past 3NF because it becomes impractical.
Index	An internal lookup table that speeds up the performance of the database. SQL Server creates a few indexes on e.g. primary keys.
Connection String	A string used in your code to get access to the server and database. It can be a pain to get right, although Visual Studio has a good wizard for this.
SQL	Structured Query Language. This is the "programming language" of the database. SQL can be kept in the client code, from where it is sent to the database to be executed, or it can stay inside the database as Stored Procedures.
T-SQL	Transaction SQL. This is Microsoft's extended SQL - with variables and flow-control.
Constraints	Rules that the database will enforce for you. Helps keep the data(base) healthy.
Join	Joining foreign and primary keys at run-time and selecting relevant columns from the resulting "extended table" is the real power of relational databases.
Transaction	A good database does all or nothing (if an error occurs midway through an operation).
Anomaly	A poorly designed database can cause anomalies when updating, inserting or deleting.

2.2 CRUD and ACID

You can always count on the programming world to come up with catchy acronyms.

CRUD REFERS TO **CREATE-RETRIEVE-UPDATE-DELETE**

This summarizes the main operations on a running database. Note that these terms are all related to data operations on existing tables - see Table 2.3. In SQL there is a CREATE command for creating tables. This is not related to the "create" in CRUD. See Table 2.3 for an explanation. If you are interested in REST-protocols, you will find similar CRUD actions in these.

Table 2.3: CRUD

CRUD	SQL	Meaning
Create	INSERT	Insert new row(s) in a database table. It is possible - but not typical - to insert more than one row per SQL-statement.
Retrieve	SELECT	Fetch any number of rows based on various criteria, grouped, sorted etc. This is the most complex command. This is where we use JOIN. To most people a *query* is what is implemented by a SELECT.
Update	UPDATE	Update selected columns. As with SELECT it is possible to work on many rows at a time.
Delete	DELETE	Delete any number of rows based on given criteria.

In order to understand some basic database concepts in this chapter we need to use the SELECT before we dig further into it in Chapter 4.

ACID REFERS TO **ATOMIC-CONSISTENT-ISOLATED-DURABLE.**

Whereas CRUD refers to the functions you use as a programmer or database-administrator, ACID refers to the implementation and quality of the RDBMS itself[1]. If we were to design such a system, we would need to

---

[1]And to a degree also to your implementation

understand these things to the bottom.

Table 2.4: ACID

ACID	Meaning
Atomic	The Greek word "atom" means "indivisible". This is implemented by a *transaction*, which is a series of actions that are either all done - or rolled back if something fails along the way.
Consistent	As programmers, or database-administrators, we are given some responsibility for keeping data consistent. This is done by *constraints*, *triggers* and *cascades* - terms we will meet later.
Isolated	This is really low-level. The RDBMS may split the SQL-command in parts to run in parallel. The order of these must not affect the result.
Durable	Once data is stored in the database they must stay - also if there is a power break-down.

2.3   OLTP versus OLAP

SQL Server is often described as an advanced *OLTP* system. OLTP means *On-Line Transaction Processing* and is often mentioned as the opposite of *OLAP - On-Line Analytical Processing*. In both cases "on-line" is mostly a marketing term saying that answers are fast. The point is whether the system is *transactional* or *analytical*. This relates not only to the design of your database, but also to the design of the entire RDBMS[2]. OLTP-systems are used in e.g. web-stores and other *POS* - Point of Sales - applications, as well as in production and administration. Data-mining and data-warehouse systems on the other hand, are typically of the OLAP-type.

You could say that OLTP is designed for many users doing many small writes, whereas OLAP is designed for fewer users doing many large reads. When you are writing to a database, it is very important to protect the system against something failing "midair" which could lead to inconsistent data - hence the focus on transactions in OLTP. This is not so relevant in

---

[2]OLAP databases are sometimes not even relational and thus not RDBMSs

OLAP, where the focus is on fast and efficient reads on more static data. Writing may not take place at all.

You can also say that OLTP is for daily business - executing the current strategy, while OLAP is for analyzing historical data and thus helps create tomorrow's strategy. A company may use traditional OLTP in sales & production. Later data is copied to an OLAP system where it is *not* normalized (we will get back to this shortly). Here it is analyzed for more strategic purposes.

Traditional RDBMSs like SQL Server, Oracle and MySQL are all of the OLTP kind.

2.4 Keys

When a database is in *first normal form* (*1NF*) or higher, each row is unique as we shall see when we discuss *normalization*. The *primary key* in a table is the single thing needed to define & find a unique row. When the primary keys from table A are used in table B they are said to be *foreign keys* in table B. This is because they refer back to table A. The primary/foreign key *relationship* is the main vehicle of *joins*.

2.4.1 Management Studio and Keys

Figure 2.1 is generated with the help of Management Studio's *diagram function*, on a web-shop database called "Shop". This is called an *entity-relation* (ER) diagram, simply because tables are entities and the keys provide the relations. Here the names of the columns are written horizontally - more practical for text. I have given the auto-generated diagram a little help by moving the endpoints of all primary/foreign key relationships to the relevant column-names. Each relationship has a (yellow) key at the primary key end, and an "infinity symbol" (∞) at the foreign key end. This signifies a *one-to-many* (1:n) relation - in other words that a specific key value can occur only once as a primary key, but many times as a foreign key.

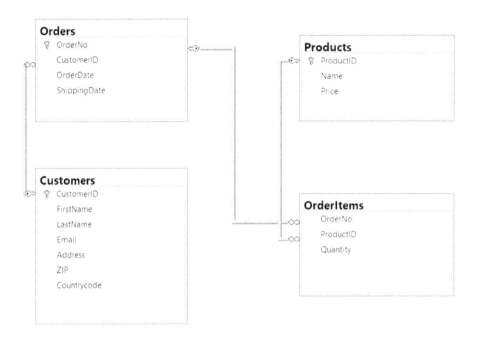

Figure 2.1: Keys and relationships in Shop

In the Shop system one ProductID belongs to a single product in Products, but may appear in many rows in OrderItems, since many people may buy the same product.

It is relatively easy to tell Management Studio that a column is to be a primary key. In Table-Design, you right-click the relevant column-name and click on "Set Primary Key". This can also be written in a script.

One way to appoint a foreign key via the IDE is to expand the table in the *Object Explorer*, then right-click on "Keys" and select "New Foreign Key". Figure 2.2 shows how the "Foreign Key Relationships" dialog appears when adding a foreign key to OrderItems. The dialog starts out with a new relationship called FK_OrderItems_OrderItems - a self-referencing relation.[3] Now "Tables and Columns Specific" is expanded, the ellipsis (...) box is clicked, and the "Tables and Columns" dialog is shown on top. Now select the tables and columns for the primary and foreign key, and change the name of the relations accordingly. Remember to save all the way out.

---

[3]You cannot cancel out of this dialog! If needed, delete this relation, then press "Close".

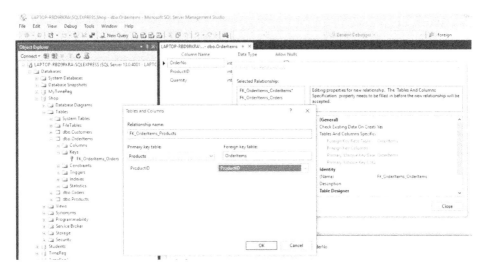

Figure 2.2: Adding a Foreign Key

Figure 2.1 as well as Figure 2.2 both show that I have chosen to use the same name - ProductID - for the primary and foreign keys at both ends of the relationship. This is a good habit - albeit not a must, which is also practical when you realize that e.g. a ManagerID in a table of departments is actually the same as the EmployeeID in a table of employees.

2.4.2 Composite Keys

Sometimes a key is defined as the *composite* of several columns. Imagine a database in a TV-factory. Each TV is registered here. We cannot simply use the serial-number of the TV as key, since serial-numbers normally are only unique for a given type-number or name. In this case we will define the primary key to be the composite of type-number/name and serial-number. If the factory manufactures TVs for several vendors, the key would need to also include a VendorID or similar.

2.4.3 Natural and Surrogate Keys

The TV-factory example is a good case for the use of *natural keys* - business domain integers and strings.

Mostly I try to avoid the use of natural keys. Examples are phone-numbers, network-names, license-plates, salary-numbers etc. These *are* unique - but they still might change. Surely people change phone-numbers, but they also change their name (e.g. when marrying) and thus get a new network-name. If a person is hired as e.g. a student-help, and then later hired "for real" it may change the salary-number. I prefer to have a "behind-the-scenes" innocent running-number - totally detached from the real world. This is a *surrogate key*.

Using a surrogate key, I keep all other attributes as plain columns, and can change them as needed. A minor downside to the use of a surrogate key is that when it is used as foreign key in another table, you need to make the join to have any use of it, whereas a natural key might carry information by itself.

An example is a table of departments containing a manager as a foreign key, referencing the manager in the Employees table. If the managers network-name is the (natural) key, you may recognize this when looking at the Departments table. On the other hand, if you only see an integer ID, you need to join data with the Employees table, in order to learn more. Often that join is needed anyway, in order to get to other columns.

In Figure 2.1 I have used keys that are post-fixed "ID" when they are surrogates. I consider OrderNo a natural key since it will be used on the invoice. This may create gaps in the order numbers if customers bail out before completing the order. If the taxman[4] starts wondering about these gaps, it is an indication that I should have used a surrogate OrderID and that OrderNo should be a non-key column, incremented only for orders that made it all the way through the web-shop.

Note that such an incrementing number can be a problem for an application. If multiple instances of the application simultaneously - on behalf of several users - try to read a number, add one and use the new number at the same time[5], it may give cause to *race* issues. The database on the other hand typically has a way to increment numbers *atomically* - the "A" in ACID - as we shall see in Subsection 2.4.4. So - if possible - leave this to the database.

---

[4]Thanks to the Beatles for this term - makes more sense than "IRS-employee"
[5]This is known as Read-Modify-Write

In the TimeReg-sample, we shall see that it is practical to create a project without an official project number, as this might come later from another source. If - and when - this becomes available, it is written in the relevant non-key column.

2.4.4 Identity

Most RDBMSs - including SQL Server - have support for an *identity* column. This is very practical for use as surrogate keys. By definition these can stand alone - they are not part of a composite key. In SQL Server identity-based values are initialized with a *seed* - initial value - as well as an increment value. By default, both are 1, so that the rows in the identity-column are numbered 1,2,3,4 etc. Whenever a row is deleted, a gap remains. For this reason the application software cannot assume that e.g. the latest given ID can be used as an indication of the number of rows. Identity-based keys are used a lot in this book, as we will clearly see in the various T-SQL scripts.

If a new database is created as a clone by restoring a backup of another base, and then deleting the contents, the identity will continue where it "left off". The following line will reset the key - in this case on the "Main" table in the TimeReg base that we will see later. Do not do this on a non-empty base!

```
DBCC CHECKIDENT ('[TimeReg].[dbo].[Main]', RESEED,0);
```

2.5 Normalization

Edward Codd, the inventor of the relational database, described the process of *normalization*. He described a number of *normal forms* - starting with 1'st Normal Form (1NF), stepping up to Fifth Normal Form (5NF) - with each step including the rules of the previous, plus more. Later "Boyce-Codd Normal Form" was introduced between 3NF and 4NF. Normally 3NF is enough to avoid problems, and going further can cause performance problems. A popular summary of the first three normal forms goes like this:

Every non-key column in a table should depend on the key, the whole key, and nothing but the key, so help me Codd.

In Table 2.5 the above sentence is split into phrases. Each describes the relevant normalization rules.

Table 2.5: Normalization

NF	Phrase	Description
1NF	The Key	There is a unique primary key, based on the least number of columns needed. Each cell is "atomic", meaning that it contains a single value - e.g. not a list of values. Finally, repeating columns like e.g. Student1, Student2, Student3...are not allowed.
2NF	The Whole Key	1NF is obeyed and all non-key columns depend fully on the entire key.
3NF	Nothing but the Key	2NF is obeyed and all non-keys depend only on the key

2.5.1 Case: Students Database

Let us try a simple and classic case. We will discuss normalization and try out some T-SQL in Management Studio. Table 2.6 is a single-table database of students. Single-table databases are often referred to as *flat databases*. If you keep your data in Excel, this is a flat "database". When this is moved to a real database there is a risk that the structure stays the same.

The Students database and table can be created via the GUI in Management Studio, but once the database is created[6], you might want to add the table by typing the *T-SQL* in Listing 2.1 in a "New Query" window, followed by F5 for execution.

Note that the *GO* keyword is used like a "batch" termination. If variables are used, they go out of scope after GO. If GO is followed by an integer, the batch is repeated this number of times. This makes no sense here, but may be used with INSERT to quickly generate a lot of dummy data.

---

[6]The creation of the database can also be scripted

Listing 2.1: Create Table

```
1  CREATE TABLE dbo.Students
2  (
3      StudentNo  int          NOT NULL,
4      FirstName  nvarchar(50)  NOT NULL,
5      LastName   nvarchar(50)  NOT NULL,
6      Class      nvarchar(50)  NOT NULL,
7  )
8  GO
```

Listing 2.2: Delete Table

```
1  DROP TABLE dbo.Students
2  GO
```

If you don't like the result of the "CREATE TABLE" it is easy to delete it. If you type and execute the script in Listing 2.2 in another query window, it is easy to go back and forth between the windows and experiment.

Table 2.6 is not even 1NF since the "Classes" clearly may contain a list of values as is the case with Peter - student 401.

Table 2.6: Students database - non-normalized

StudentNo	FirstName	LastName	Classes
401	Peter	Anderson	Basic Math, Adv. Physics
402	John	Grey	History
403	Joan	Cooper	Basic Math
404	Annie	Dawson	Adv. Physics

We could fix the problem by introducing more columns - like "Class 1", "Class 2" etc. However, this is another violation of 1NF. Instead, we can have one row per student per class - as in Table 2.7. Now we have no lists in any column, and we have no repeating columns. This is a classic Excel solution. It is also 1NF.

Table 2.7: Students database - 1NF

StudentNo	FirstName	LastName	Class
401	Peter	Anderson	Basic Math
401	Peter	Anderson	Adv. Physics
402	John	Grey	History
403	Joan	Cooper	Basic Math
404	Annie	Dawson	Adv. Physics

Should we now decide that it is a good idea - with the existing data - to make StudentNo a primary key in Management Studio, we get the following error when trying to save the design change with F5:

'Students' table - Unable to create index 'PK_Students'. The CREATE UNIQUE INDEX statement terminated because a duplicate key was found for the object name 'dbo.Students' and the index name 'PK_Students'. The duplicate key value is (401). Could not create constraint or index. See previous errors. The statement has been terminated.

Now that's what I call a great error-message. We do not have a primary key in StudentNo as it must be unique. However, if you try to define a composite primary key in the Students table, based on StudentNo *and* Class, you actually get away with it. This supports that the Students table can be said to be 1NF - as ugly as it is. It does not qualify as 2NF, as the rule "all non-key columns depend on the *entire* key" is not obeyed. The name of the student depends on the StudentNo, but not on the Class.

The composite key can be created in the GUI by using "Set Primary Key" on both column names before executing (F5). Alternatively the composite key can be created in T-SQL - this time ALTERing the existing table as in Listing 2.3.

Listing 2.3: Alter Table

```
1  ALTER TABLE Students
2  ADD CONSTRAINT PK_Students PRIMARY KEY CLUSTERED
3  (
4      StudentNo, Class
5  )
6  GO
```

When a primary key is based on a single column, the text "PRIMARY

KEY" can be a modifier on the line with the relevant column in the Create Table script. If the key is composite you can do something similar by writing `PRIMARY KEY` (Key1, Key2). In either case, the "CONSTRAINT" way to specify it also works.

2.5.2 Script Table

Management Studio allows you to right-click the table (and actually the whole database) and select "Script Table As...". Thus, it is possible to perform something in the UI first, and then study the T-SQL afterwards. This is how Listing 2.4 was created.

Listing 2.4: Result of Script Table

```
1   USE [Students]
2   GO
3
4   /****** Object:  Table [dbo].[Students]    **/
5   SET ANSI_NULLS ON
6   GO
7
8   SET QUOTED_IDENTIFIER ON
9   GO
10
11  CREATE TABLE [dbo].[Students](
12      StudentNo int          NOT NULL,
13      FirstName nvarchar(50) NOT NULL,
14      LastName  nvarchar(50) NOT NULL,
15      Class     nvarchar(50) NOT NULL,
16   CONSTRAINT [PK_students] PRIMARY KEY CLUSTERED
17  (
18      [StudentNo] ASC,
19      [Class] ASC
20  )WITH (PAD_INDEX = OFF, STATISTICS_NORECOMPUTE = OFF,
21  IGNORE_DUP_KEY = OFF, ALLOW_ROW_LOCKS = ON,
22  ALLOW_PAGE_LOCKS = ON) ON [PRIMARY]
23  ) ON [PRIMARY]
24
25  GO
```

There is a lot to note in the output:

❒ The first line is "[USE Students]". It defines the scope - the name of the database, which incidentally is also called "Students". It is advisable to use that in input as well, to avoid messing with the wrong database.

❏ The script is based on a "CREATE TABLE". It is also possible to have it generated as an "ALTER TABLE" script.

❏ The output is filled with "[]" brackets. These are delimiters that are needed if a name contains a space, a reserved symbol or a keyword. They are optional in the input if none of these symbols are used.

❏ The lines starting with "SET", as well as the assignments in the "WITH" part, contain a number of defaults. We see e.g. that if a row is being updated, SQL Server will lock access to it from other users. This is one way to handle the "atomic" requirement in ACID. Locking strategies are an important part of database implementations, however, we can go very far with the defaults.

❏ "ON [PRIMARY]" is not related to the primary key, but to a low-level default file specification. We do not need to specify this in our scripts.

2.5.3   Anomalies

If we decide to avoid abbreviations and change "Adv. Physics" to "Advanced Physics", we will need to update in several places. This is an *update anomaly*. Also, should John Grey decide to quit, we have no traces of the class in History anymore. This is a *delete anomaly*. Finally, if we want to introduce the class "Religion" we have to wait for a student taking this class before we can introduce it. This is an *insert anomaly*.

In my experience, programmers are very much aware of the Update Anomaly. Programmers hate repeated text-strings. We long to define them "constant" in one way or another. This instinct also helps a little with the other anomalies.

2.5.4   Association Tables

There are situations where the programmer's normal thinking is no help. We tend to work with collections, and collections of collections. That is not how databases are designed. Take the Shop system from Figure 2.1. A programmer with no database experience would think that an Order has many OrderItems. 1NF tells us that we cannot have OrderItem1,

OrderItem2 etc. as columns in Orders table. The programmers first instinct is to have a reference to an OrderList - another table. Unfortunately, this would mean that each different row in Orders should have its own table with OrderItems - dynamically created as orders are created. That is exactly how programs work with collections, but it is not how databases are organized.

Instead, the relation is turned upside down, and we have one big table of OrderItems referring back to the Orders table. And to the Products table. This way of handling m:n relations is called an *association table*. An association table has rows with foreign keys only - no primary keys. Non-key columns as our Quantity may occur. Note that sometimes association tables are called *junction tables*.

2.5.5 Students Database 3NF

The use of an association table is also the solution to our Students case. Instead of a single table we now have three - see Tables 2.8, 2.9 and 2.10. StudentNo and ClassID are now primary keys in respectively the first and the second of these tables, while they are both foreign keys in the third.

Table 2.8: Students database - 3NF - Students Table

StudentNo	FirstName	LastName
401	Peter	Anderson
402	John	Grey
403	Joan	Cooper
404	Annie	Dawson

Table 2.9: Students database - 3NF - Class Table

ClassID	Class
1	Basic Math
2	Advanced Math
3	Basic Physics
4	Advanced Physics
5	History

Table 2.10: Students database - 3NF - Associations

StudentNo	ClassID
401	1
401	4
402	5
403	1
404	4

2.5.6   Order System 3NF

Returning to the Order system from Figure 2.1, we see that it satisfies 1NF
- except maybe for the Address column in the Customers table. The (street)
Address column is probably made up by several strings like street-name,
street-number etc. When is an address a list of values, and when is it
atomic? The jury is still out on this one. We have already taken ZIP and
country-code out as separate columns. Should street-no and floor-no and
maybe apartment number also be columns of their own? Clearly the street
address can be broken down, but this process requires us to foresee all
sorts of addressing schemes. Is it really worth it? Probably not. If we
accept the (street) Address as being "atomic", 1NF is satisfied.

The Order system also satisfies 2NF as all non-key columns depend on
the (whole) key in all tables. Is 3NF also satisfied? Yes, in all tables the
non-key columns depend on "nothing but the key".

I once used a database-interface to "Altium", which is a computer-aided-
design program. The interface supplies Altium with a list of electronic
components. This table can contain hundred-thousands of rows. For each
row there is the expected "Component Type", "Unit", "Value" and other
columns, but there are also columns like "Manufacturer1", "Manufac-
turer2" etc. This violates 1NF. The most annoying consequence was that
we were limited on the number of manufacturers (and similar attributes).
Probably Altium had chosen this layout to make life easy for all those that
imported from - or continued to use - Excel. It is easy to use a flat Excel
sheet - at the cost of flexibility.

2.6 Joins

One of the most important database-concepts is the *join*. Here we "align" the primary keys from one table with their specific foreign key counterparts from another table - generating a new wider, temporary table. There are a number of different ways to do this:

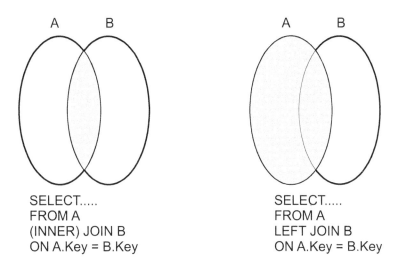

```
SELECT.....                    SELECT.....
FROM A                         FROM A
(INNER) JOIN B                 LEFT JOIN B
ON A.Key = B.Key               ON A.Key = B.Key
```

Figure 2.3: Most important Joins

❐ **Join**

In SQL, the simple *JOIN* is the same as the *INNER JOIN*. This is what we see in Figure 2.3 on the left side. The resulting temporary table created by the join consists of only elements where there are matching keys in the two tables. As there may be several foreign key instances for the same primary key, the new table can have several rows with this primary key - one for each of these instances. On the other hand, there will be no rows where a key exists only as a primary key or only as a foreign key. The latter case sounds wrong - how can there be a foreign key without a corresponding primary key? There may have been no constraint declared (we will get to this). In fact the two key-columns in the two tables may have been created totally independent of each other - not as keys - until we just decided to write the SQL JOIN statement where we treat the columns as primary/foreign keys.

❐ **Left Join**
This is sometimes known as a *left outer join*. The SQL LEFT JOIN is
seen on the right side of Figure 2.3. In this case all rows from table A
appear in the resulting temporary table. Where matching keys are
found in table B, the rows are extended with data from here. These
rows are thus identical to the rows in the (inner) join. The new stuff
here is that we also see the rows in table A that have no matches in
table B. The "missing cells" are filled with NULLs.

❐ **Right Join**
This works the same way as a left join - but now with the full B table
and the matches from A. Personally I never use a right join - I simply
reference the tables in the opposite order and use the left join.

❐ **Full Join**
This is also known as a *full outer join* and is not shown in the figure.
This includes all rows from both tables - matched when possible with
common keys, and with NULLs in the rest of the columns.

In order to demonstrate joins we will reuse the Shop system - now with
data. These data were simply written into tables 2.11 through 2.14, using
Management Studio's "Edit Top 200 Rows". In real life they are written
with an application.

Table 2.11: Orders

OrderNo	CustomerID	OrderDate	ShippingDate
1	1	2018-01-03	2018-01-06
2	1	2018-02-02	2018-02-04
3	2	2018-03-03	2018-03-06
4	4	2018-04-03	2018-04-05

Table 2.12: Products

ProductID	Name	Price
1	Round Table oak	1999
2	Round Table mahogany	2299
3	Square Table white	1699
4	Chair black	599
5	Chair white	599
6	Chair red	599
7	Wall-Lamp	350
8	Ceiling-Lamp	299

Table 2.13: Order-Items is an association table

OrderNo	ProductID	Quantity
1	2	2
1	3	1
2	4	4
2	3	1
2	1	1
3	5	2
4	2	1

Table 2.14: Customers

CustomerID	FirstName	LastName	Email	Address	ZIP	Countrycode
1	John	Drake	jd@gmail.com	Savsvinget 7	2230	DK
2	Niels	Petersen	nielsp@hotmail.com	Kobbervejen 8a	2700	DK
3	Pia	Hansen	ph@hansen.dk	Roskildevej 55	3400	DK
4	Linda	Jones	ljones@gmail.com	Smørhult 9	4790	SE
5	Carl	Nielsen	cn@hotmail.com	Violinvej 22	5600	DK

Now for the join. The following T-SQL queries may be written in Management Studio's Query Editor. You may need to start all the following T-SQL scripts with the following to set the right scope:

```
USE Shop
Go
```

Oftentimes examples start with "SELECT *". The star is an easy way to get data from all columns in the table. The names used in the output corresponds to the table column names. It is however not a good habit to use the star in real applications. Table-changes may lead to columns appearing in another order.

Another reason for specifically naming columns, instead of using the star, is to limit the output - as in Listing 2.5. The join effectively generates a new temporary table with all columns from all the joined tables. This means that the key columns are shown in all their occurrences - as primary keys and as foreign keys. Normally you only want to see a single instance, or maybe none if they are surrogate keys. The resulting table here is so wide, that not only are the keys not shown - the table is also scaled down to fit the page. Finally, the "AS"in the SELECT renames the output column headers - in this case to shorter names.

Listing 2.5: Joins

```
1   SELECT Orders.OrderNo AS No, OrderDate, ShippingDate,
2       Quantity AS Qty, FirstName AS First, LastName AS Last,
3       Email, Address, ZIP, CountryCode AS Ctry, Name, Price
4   FROM Orders
5       JOIN OrderItems ON
6           OrderItems.OrderNo = Orders.OrderNo
7       JOIN Customers ON
8           Orders.CustomerID  = Customers.CustomerID
9       JOIN Products ON
10          Products.ProductID = OrderItems.ProductID
```

Table 2.15: Joined tables.

No	OrderDate	ShippingDate	Qty	First	Last	Email	Address	ZIP	Ctry	Name	Price
1	2018-01-03	2018-01-06	2	John	Drake	jd@gmail.com	Savsvinget 7	2230	DK	Round Table mahogany	2299
1	2018-01-03	2018-01-06	1	John	Drake	jd@gmail.com	Savsvinget 7	2230	DK	Square Table white	1699
2	2018-02-02	2018-02-04	4	John	Drake	jd@gmail.com	Savsvinget 7	2230	DK	Chair black	599
2	2018-02-02	2018-02-04	1	John	Drake	jd@gmail.com	Savsvinget 7	2230	DK	Square Table white	1699
2	2018-02-02	2018-02-04	1	John	Drake	jd@gmail.com	Savsvinget 7	2230	DK	Round Table oak	1999
3	2018-03-03	2018-03-06	2	Niels	Petersen	nielsp@hotmail.com	Kobbervejen 8a	2700	DK	Chair white	599
4	2018-04-03	2018-04-05	1	Linda	Jones	ljones@gmail.com	Smørhult 9	4790	SE	Round Table mahogany	2299

Note how the output from the join looks very much like an Excel solution in a flat table would look from the start. In other words: we start with a flat table, which we normalize into several tables. Then we join them back to a flat table. The main advantage in the well-normalized database is that it is much easier to maintain - no anomalies.

When doing an (inner) join we get the *intersection* of the tables - only the rows where keys match in all the joined tables. To demonstrate the difference between (inner) join and left join we need to start with a table that is not fully "used" by the other tables. The Products table is a good example. First an (inner) join is performed again. Note the use of "SELECT *" and how this results in column names as in the original tables, and that the keys appear both as primary and as foreign keys. Then the same query is done - except this time with a left join.

Listing 2.6: Inner Join

```
1  SELECT *
2  FROM Products
3    JOIN OrderItems ON
4    Products.ProductID = OrderItems.ProductID
```

Table 2.16: Inner Join of Products and OrderItems

ProductID	Name	Price	OrderNo	ProductID	Quantity
2	Round Table mahogany	2299	1	2	2
3	Square Table white	1699	1	3	1
4	Chair black	599	2	4	4
3	Square Table white	1699	2	3	1
1	Round Table oak	1999	2	1	1
5	Chair white	599	3	5	2
2	Round Table mahogany	2299	4	2	1

Listing 2.7: Left Join

```
1  SELECT *
2  FROM Products
3    LEFT JOIN OrderItems ON
4    Products.ProductID = OrderItems.ProductID
```

Table 2.17: Left Join of Products and OrderItems

ProductID	Name	Price	OrderNo	ProductID	Quantity
1	Round Table oak	1999	2	1	1
2	Round Table mahogany	2299	1	2	2
2	Round Table mahogany	2299	4	2	1
3	Square Table white	1699	1	3	1
3	Square Table white	1699	2	3	1
4	Chair black	599	2	4	4
5	Chair white	599	3	5	2
6	Chair red	599	NULL	NULL	NULL
7	Wall-Lamp	350	NULL	NULL	NULL
8	Ceiling-Lamp	299	NULL	NULL	NULL

As described earlier - when doing an inner join we get the *intersection* - the rows where keys match in all the joined tables. In the original tables there were no NULL values. Thus, there are no NULL values in the (inner) joined table. With the left join we get all rows from the Products (left) table, with matching rows from OrderItems (right) table. Since there are products that are not sold, the corresponding rows now contain NULL values for the OrderItem columns.

We also see that the rows that are common to both outputs are not in the same order. SQL guarantees nothing about row order - unless you specify it. We will see this in Chapter 4.

2.7   Data Types and NULL

Table 2.18 shows the most common data-types used in T-SQL. There are four types of strings - with and without unicode, and with fixed or dynamic spacing. The reason for the strange 'n' in e.g. "nchar" is that it originally meant "National" chars. The *real* type corresponds to a classic *float* in C-type languages, whereas the T-SQL "float" (without a size-specifier) corresponds to a C-type *double*.

Later we shall see that the TimeReg sample uses the *datetime* format a lot. That might not come as a surprise, however datetime takes up 8 bytes for every timestamp, where 3 is enough for storing a relevant *date* without time. When I designed the physical layer (we will get back to this in Section 3.4) it was not clear whether a need to compare timestamps on the same date would arise, so I went for the safe solution. This has influenced the C# code as well, and thus a clean-up is probably not going to happen.

We know zero-values like the empty string and the value 0 for an integer. These are legal values specific for the type. This is different from NULL, which is "missing" or "unknown" value - much like a null-pointer in OOP. NULL is necessary in the following scenarios:

 ❐ An outer join as we saw earlier in Table 2.17. In this case we extend existing rows with columns from another table. In e.g. the left join we will have rows in the left table without matching values in the right table - but we want to show something anyway. NULL makes sense. It is however possible to specify default values to use - in the SQL join statement.

❐ INSERT SQL statements may be performed with values for only some columns. What to do with the rest? If the table was created with default values for the relevant columns, these are used. Otherwise, NULL is used.

Table 2.18: T-SQL Selected data types

T-SQL	.Net	Meaning
bigint	Int64	8 Bytes Signed Integer.
int	Int32	4 Bytes Signed Integer.
bit	Boolean	True/False.
real	Single	4 Bytes classic C "float".
float	Double	8 Bytes classic C "double".
date	-	3 Bytes. Year 1-9999.
datetime	DateTime	8 Bytes. Year 1753-9999 & fractions of seconds.
datetime2	DateTime	6-8 Bytes. Year 1-9999 & fractions of seconds.
char(n)	Byte Array	n bytes fixed storage. Note that by default strings are padded with spaces.
varchar(n)	Byte Array	Used bytes (max n) + 2 dynamic storage. May use less space than char, but slower to address.
nchar(n)	String	2*n bytes fixed storage - padded with spaces.
nvarchar(n)	String	2*(used bytes) +2 dynamic storage. May use less space than nchar, but slower to address.

Handling NULL values can be problematic. It makes life a little easier if default values are defined for all columns. These are used in INSERTs, but not in the outer join scenario. Sometimes the *null-coalescing* C# operator "??" comes in handy. It tests a variable for null. It can be used together with types that are made "nullable" by postfixing with "?". See Listing 2.8.

Listing 2.8: Nullable data types

```
1   int? x = null;   // x may be NULL or an int
2
3   // Set y equal to x if not NULL - else use 0
4   int y = x ?? 0;
```

Note that the types in SQL Server are listed in Management Studio under the catalog in the path: Programmability-Types-System Data Types.

2.8   Integrity and Constraints

The RDBMS will check that primary keys are unique. This is called *entity integrity*. When natural candidates for keys are not used as such, it may be wise to explicitly introduce a UNIQUE *constraint*. This can specify that e.g. a salary-number must be unique.

It is also important to assure that a specific row with a given primary key cannot be deleted as long as there is a foreign key in another table relating to it. Similarly, you should not be allowed to create a foreign key without a matching primary key. This is called *referential integrity*. Modern RDBMSs enforce this through constraints. If a constraint is not created, you are responsible for this enforcement in your client code. As there can be more clients to the same database, each client needs to do this check. Surely a constraint in the database is preferred.

The RDBMS can handle an unlawful delete in two ways: Either it does not perform the delete, but returns an error. Or it deletes the row with the primary key, and also all rows that relates to it via a foreign key. This is known as a *cascade*, and is something you set up in the "Foreign Key Relationships" dialog from Figure 2.2.

If the RDBMS is designed correct, it has taken ACID into consideration. The "C" in ACID is "consistency", and while the basic tables may be consistent on their own, it is your responsibility to assure consistency between tables, preferably using the above concepts. On top of this there is also consistency requirements on the application level. This we will come back to when we get to C#.

As stated, we sometimes want to enforce uniqueness on one or more columns that are not part of a key.

I will go a little ahead of myself and use an association table called "MyProjects", that is created as part of the TimeReg project as an example. In this table we have rows that contain two foreign keys - one is ID for Employees and the other is ID for Projects. Any employee can work on any project - but it only makes sense to have one row for any relevant combination. We want the database to enforce this constraint.

This is a little hard to find in Management Studio - and not very logical, since you end up with something in the object tree under keys and indexes - not under constraints. Let's walk through it:

① Right-click on the table where you want the constraint.

② Select Design in the popup-menu.

③ Right-click left to the table in the Designer - where you also select and see keys.

④ In the popup-menu select "Indexes/keys...".

⑤ A dialog appears - see Figure 2.4. In this dialog, change the Type from "Index" to "Unique Key". Although it is called "Unique Key" it is not what we normally call a key.

⑥ You may also change the name - "Unique_MyProjects" is used in the figure.

⑦ Click on the field next to Columns and an ellipsis (...) appears. Click on this and now the "Index Columns" dialog appears.

⑧ Now select the columns that together must be unique.

⑨ OK, Close and Save.

To see the consequence of the above, we can ask Management Studio to "Script the table". The resulting T-SQL is found in Listing 2.9. Aside from the long list of defaults given, the syntax is not hard to understand. Note that the foreign key constraints are not shown here.

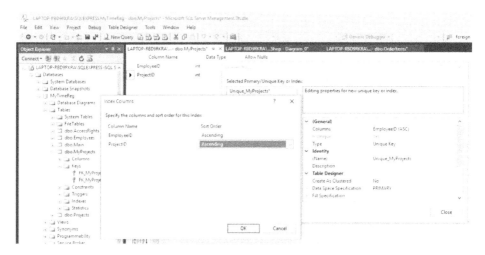

Figure 2.4: Set up a Unique Constraint

Listing 2.9: Create table with constraint

```
1   CREATE TABLE [dbo].[MyProjects](
2         [EmployeeID] [int] NOT NULL,
3         [ProjectID]  [int] NOT NULL,
4    CONSTRAINT [Unique_MyProjects] UNIQUE NONCLUSTERED
5   (
6         [EmployeeID] ASC,
7         [ProjectID]  ASC
8   )WITH (PAD_INDEX = OFF, STATISTICS_NORECOMPUTE = OFF,
9      IGNORE_DUP_KEY = OFF, ALLOW_ROW_LOCKS = ON,
10     ALLOW_PAGE_LOCKS = ON) ON [PRIMARY]
11  ) ON [PRIMARY]
```

The last type of integrity is *domain integrity* where SQL Server is configured to CHECK that values in a column are e.g. within a specified range. This is pretty much like parameter checking in a program.

The whole CHECK stuff can be quite confusing. You might actually see text like WITH CHECK CHECK.

CHECK enables a constraint while NOCHECK disables a constraint that would otherwise automatically be applied.

"WITH CHECK" is used when a constraint is added, to tell SQL Server that existing values must also abide to the CHECK. If this fails, you get an error and must sort out the problem and try again. "WITH NOCHECK" means that the constraint only applies for new values.

Chapter 3

TimeReg Database

3.1   Introduction

I have tried to make TimeReg not only for top management. Project managers can analyze time-consumption on subprojects, and developers can manage their vacation etc. You may download the sample, complete with a small sample database, and use it while you read the book. Or you may simply read the text and continue.

3.2   TimeReg Requirements

Basically the requirement for the TimeReg application was something like:

The daily reporting of hours on projects must be simple, as this is the most common operation. This could e.g. be in a week-based form - pretty much like the timetable school-children has. Somehow it would be nice if not just hours is noted, but also a free-text comment. Users should only see whatever projects they have previously selected as relevant - "My Projects"- not other peoples projects. All users must be able to create simple reports directly in the program. It must be easy to save these in an Excel-friendly format. Only managers are allowed to see other employees sickness and vacation. A project-manager should be able to easily see accumulated numbers on sub-parts of a project. We want to be able to break down the work on a project into the individuals or departments that delivered the work. The program should be able to automatically transfer hours on customer-specific projects to another, Oracle-based, database from where billing is already done (not included in the sample).

Figure 3.1 shows a PowerPoint version of the main view requirements, created for a review within the management team. It may not be the best way to demonstrate a user-interface, but the point is that it was easy to create. Compare this to Figure 1.1, which shows the resulting program, and you will find that the simple PowerPoint does a pretty neat job.

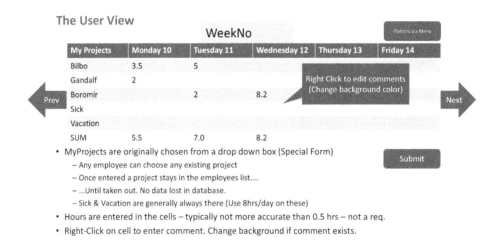

Figure 3.1: PowerPoint Requirement Spec for main view

3.3 Logical Design

Databases are designed top-down. There is a High-Level design in which the main entities (tables) are found and relations are defined, based on the business model. Then there is a low-level design where data-types, indexes, constraints and views etc are found. All these things we will get back to in Chapter 4. These two levels are often called respectively *logical design* and *physical design*. Coming from the world of hardware and embedded software, I find the term "physical design" confusing, but it is commonly used. So let's get on with the logical design of TimeReg:

Look at the requirements. Try all nouns as candidates for entities (tables). Then all attributes for these as columns in the table. The individual items then become the rows.

The following nouns are found in the requirements for the sample: Time-Registration, Employees, Projects, Sub-part of project, Departments, Comments, Hours, Weeks, Users, Vacation, Sickness, Reports, Managers, Operation, Numbers, Individual, Work. We will take them one-by-one:

❐ **Time-Registration**
   This is the overall purpose and thus is not a table, but the entire system.

❐ **Employees**
   This is a good candidate for a table. This table must contain all relevant information that pertains to the specific employee - e.g. netname, salary-number (employee number) and department (see below). I decided to use an identity surrogate key called "EmployeeID" in order to be independent of people changing names etc. I might have used the salary-number, however, I suspected that there might be people without such - e.g. consultants or students.

❐ **Department**
   This is an interesting case. As stated above, Department is chosen as an attribute of (column in) the Employees table. This is definitely in the gray-zone. If there is a Department without Employees we cannot see it. In fact, we cannot simply insert a new Department - we need to add an Employee within the Department to get it into the database. This is the *insert anomaly*. What is wrong? Department is a non-key column. According to 2NF these columns must depend on what the primary key identifies. Does the Department depend on the Employee? No - at least not in a database-technical sense.

   It would be correct to have a foreign key in the Employees table, with a relation to a primary key in a Departments table. That would make it a key-column instead of a non-key column. We would satisfy 2NF, and with a Departments table we would be able to insert departments before staffing them - no insertion anomaly. In this case it makes little sense - should such an empty department exist, there would be no hours to register anyway, and we don't care. So for the sake of simplicity - and performance - Department became a column in Employees.

Later in the TimeReg project I needed a drop-down list of departments in order to allow managers to filter on the work sourced by their own department. Lacking a Departments table, I did not have such list. This is the only time a had to resort to the *DISTINCT* SQL keyword, that traverses a table and gives a list of all unique values in a given column. In a larger system, this would not be performance optimal.

❐ **Projects**
Another good candidate for a table. Projects have attributes that become columns - like their number in various external systems and a name. A surrogate identity key - "ProjectID" - is introduced. This allows projects to be created independent of various formal number-systems. These may be assigned later, or not at all. This allows a department-manager to have tasks that are not really official projects - like tool-support. As the system became more formalized, a ManagerID was later introduced along with specific access rights.

❐ **Sub-Parts of Projects**
Project-managers like to see statistics for sub-parts of a project. I decided that a project could be a child of another project - but only one level. No grandparents. To handle this, a "Parent" column is introduced. This holds the ProjectID of the parent project. ProjectID is an identity and thus normally 1 or greater. If this is less than 1 in Parent, the project is a parent. I decided to use 0 for "normal" parent projects and -1 for special projects that only are included in visible exports when these are performed by managers. These projects are typically Vacation and Holidays. This self-referencing later made queries much more complex than otherwise necessary - as we shall see.

❐ **My Projects**
This is another interesting case. Since every employee might work on a multitude of projects, we would need to introduce an unknown amount of ProjectID columns in the Employee table if this is where we store the projects for a given employee. This would break 1NF. The exact same problem arises if we want to store all relevant EmployeeIDs for each project in the Projects table. The problem is that we do not have a 1:n relation, but an m:n relation. The solution to

this problem is an association (or junction) table - "MyProjects". This table only holds two columns: a foreign key with a ProjectID and a ditto with EmployeeID. There may be many rows with the same of either of the foreign keys, but only one with a given pair - a good case for a constraint, as described previously. In this case we only have two columns, but association tables can have more.

❒ **Operation**
This relates to the manual input of time-data and is no candidate for a table.

❒ **Report**
This might sound like a candidate for a table, but as this is the output of calculations (typically sums) it should not be a table in our database, but the result of one or more SQL operations on data in the database. The TimeReg database is *transactional* - by far the most common action performed, is typing in new hours. If this was a rare thing, while reports were done all the time, we would say that it was *analytic*. In such a case calculated data might actually go into tables for performance reasons - saving a lot of joins in the SELECT statements. That would involve the use of *triggers* for updating the sums when new data is entered - something that we don't need in this design.[1] This relates to the OLTP versus OLAP discussion.

❒ **Users**
This is the same as "employees" and "individuals". The term "developers" was also used as this was an R&D Department.

❒ **Managers**
This might seem to be a new table, but managers are also employees. In this case I decided to have a binary column in the Employees table called "SuperUser", as I (correctly) suspected that certain employees in HR or Finance might be given the same rights as managers.

❒ **Hours**
This is yet a candidate for a table. In the end I decided that Hours was the name of the most important attribute. Instead, I called the table "Main". The reason for this name is that this table becomes "the mother of all tables", being the only table that has many daily inserts. Like with Projects and Employees, a surrogate primary key is used - "MainID". Main has foreign keys for EmployeeID and ProjectID.

---

[1]Reconsider your design if triggers are needed.

❐ **Accumulated Numbers**
As described above this is generated on the fly as part of a Report.

❐ **Comment**
The comments clearly follow the hours into the Main table as a column of its own.

❐ **Week**
Here is a good example of a requirement that relates to the way data are shown on the user interface rather than to the database itself. However, hours are registered on specific dates. We do need "Date" as a column in the Main (hours) table.

❐ **Form**
Relates to the user interface.

Figure 3.2 shows how the initial table layout was drawn in PowerPoint. It just goes to show that you can get far by simple means.

Figure 3.3 shows the same tables in a diagram recently created by Management Studio. Note the added relationship from Projects to Employees. This is created by the later added ManagerID which is a foreign key matching the primary key EmployeeID in the Employees table. Other new columns in the Projects table are "GroupTag" and "Category". These are both used to organize the projects in various ways, in order for statistics to be more usable. The Category column is used by the Project Managers, while the GroupTag is used by top management. "PSONumber" is the project-number in another administrative system (from the "project sales office"). Finally, we have "InOracle" which contains the date of an export into an official Oracle system - or NULL if not exported.

Backend Database in MS SQL-Server - Tables

MainEntry*	EmployeeID**	Date	ProjectID**	Hours	Comment	InOracle
1	2	2014-11-10	1	3.5	SC Meeting prep	2015-1-1
2	2	2014-11-10	2	2.0	Prod Stop	2015-1-1
3	2	2014-11-11	1	5.0	DSP Meeting	2015-1-1
4	2	2014-11-11	3	2.0	Design Review	Null
5	2	2014-11-12	3	8.2	Coding FTDI-driver	Null

Main

Employee ID**	ProjectID**
1	1
1	2

MyProjects

Project ID*	Name	Number	Parent	Closed	PSONum	Category
1	Bilbo		0	0		NPI
2	Gandalf		0	0		NPI
3	Boromir	003. ..	0	1	675498	PSO
4	Bilbo-DSP		1	0		NPI
5	Vacation	0	-1	0		OUT

Projects

Employee ID*	Net name	Employee Name	Employee Number	Department
1	KELK	Klaus Elk	25419	7533
2	TDC	Tom Dan Cornelius	25987	7534
3	LEGO	Leif Godtfolk	23654	7537
4	DANISCO	Dan Iscosen	24985	7538

Employees

* = Key (Autonum)
** = Foreign Key

Figure 3.2: PowerPoint Design of initial tables

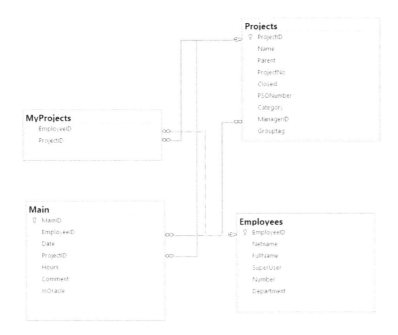

Figure 3.3: Main tables today

3.4   Physical Design

The details of the design is for now simply described by the following script, generated by SQL Server. Microsoft use the "/*..*/" comments, while I use "- -". A number of "GO" statements etc. are removed to save space.

Many of the constructs are explained in the next chapter. You may want to skip the script now and go back to it when the various concepts are described.

Listing 3.1: Result of Script Database

```
1   /****** Object:  Table [dbo].[Employees]  */
2   CREATE TABLE [dbo].[Employees](
3       -- Indentity Primary Key counting 1,2,3,4...
4       -- Note that SQL Server has NOT written 'PRIMARY' here,
5       -- but instead uses the CONSTRAINT below
6           [EmployeeID] [int] IDENTITY(1,1) NOT NULL,
7           [Netname]            [nvarchar](25) NOT NULL,
8           [FullName]           [nvarchar](50) NOT NULL,
9           [SuperUser] [bit]                NOT NULL,
10          -- Salary Number if such exists - else 0
11          [Number]     [int]               NOT NULL,
12          -- Department must be a number
13          [Department] [int]               NOT NULL,
14   CONSTRAINT [PK_Employees] PRIMARY KEY CLUSTERED
15  (
16          [EmployeeID] ASC
17  )WITH (PAD_INDEX = OFF, STATISTICS_NORECOMPUTE = OFF,
18      IGNORE_DUP_KEY = OFF, ALLOW_ROW_LOCKS = ON,
19      ALLOW_PAGE_LOCKS = ON) ON [PRIMARY]
20  ) ON [PRIMARY]
21
22  /****** Object:  Table [dbo].[Main] */
23  CREATE TABLE [dbo].[Main](
24      -- Yet an Identity Primary Key
25          [MainID]     [int] IDENTITY(1,1) NOT NULL,
26          [EmployeeID] [int]               NOT NULL,
27          [Date]       [datetime]          NOT NULL,
28          [ProjectID]  [int]               NOT NULL,
29          [Hours]      [real]              NOT NULL,
30          [Comment]    [nvarchar](200)         NULL,
31          [InOracle]   [datetime]              NULL,
32   CONSTRAINT [PK_Main] PRIMARY KEY CLUSTERED
33  (
34          [MainID] ASC
35  )WITH (PAD_INDEX = OFF, STATISTICS_NORECOMPUTE = OFF,
36      IGNORE_DUP_KEY = OFF, ALLOW_ROW_LOCKS = ON,
37      ALLOW_PAGE_LOCKS = ON) ON [PRIMARY],
38   CONSTRAINT [No_Dupl] UNIQUE NONCLUSTERED
39  (
40          [ProjectID] ASC,
```

```
41          [EmployeeID] ASC,
42          [Date] ASC
43  )WITH (PAD_INDEX = OFF, STATISTICS_NORECOMPUTE = OFF,
44      IGNORE_DUP_KEY = OFF, ALLOW_ROW_LOCKS = ON,
45      ALLOW_PAGE_LOCKS = ON) ON [PRIMARY]
46  ) ON [PRIMARY]
47
48  /****** Object:  Table [dbo].[MyProjects]  */
49  CREATE TABLE [dbo].[MyProjects](
50          [EmployeeID] [int] NOT NULL,
51          [ProjectID]  [int] NOT NULL
52  ) ON [PRIMARY]
53
54  /****** Object:  Table [dbo].[Projects]  */
55  CREATE TABLE [dbo].[Projects](
56          [ProjectID]  [int] IDENTITY(1,1) NOT NULL,
57          [Name]       [nvarchar](50)      NOT NULL,
58          [Parent]     [int]               NOT NULL,
59          [ProjectNo]  [nvarchar](50)          NULL,
60          [Closed]     [bit]               NOT NULL,
61          [PSONumber]  [int]               NOT NULL,
62          [Category]   [nvarchar](10)      NOT NULL,
63          [ManagerID]  [int]                   NULL,
64          [Grouptag]   [varchar](50)       NOT NULL,
65   CONSTRAINT [PK_Projects] PRIMARY KEY CLUSTERED
66  (
67          [ProjectID] ASC
68  )WITH (PAD_INDEX = OFF, STATISTICS_NORECOMPUTE = OFF, I
69      GNORE_DUP_KEY = OFF, ALLOW_ROW_LOCKS = ON,
70      ALLOW_PAGE_LOCKS = ON) ON [PRIMARY]
71  ) ON [PRIMARY]
72
73  ALTER TABLE [dbo].[Employees] ADD  CONSTRAINT
74    [DF_Employees_Number] DEFAULT ((0)) FOR [Number]
75  ALTER TABLE [dbo].[Employees] ADD  CONSTRAINT
76    [DF_Employees_Department] DEFAULT ((0)) FOR [Department]
77  ALTER TABLE [dbo].[Projects] ADD  CONSTRAINT
78    [DF_Projects_Closed] DEFAULT ((0)) FOR [Closed]
79  ALTER TABLE [dbo].[Projects] ADD  CONSTRAINT
80    [DF_Projects_PSONumber] DEFAULT ((0)) FOR [PSONumber]
81  ALTER TABLE [dbo].[Projects] ADD  CONSTRAINT
82  [DF_Projects_Category]  DEFAULT (N'NON') FOR [Category]
83  ALTER TABLE [dbo].[Projects] ADD  DEFAULT ('') FOR [Grouptag]
84
85  -- Here comes the constraints based on the foreign keys
86  ALTER TABLE [dbo].[Main]  WITH CHECK ADD  CONSTRAINT
87    [FK_Main_Employees] FOREIGN KEY([EmployeeID])
88  REFERENCES [dbo].[Employees] ([EmployeeID])
89
90  ALTER TABLE [dbo].[Main] CHECK CONSTRAINT [FK_Main_Employees]
91  ALTER TABLE [dbo].[Main]  WITH CHECK ADD  CONSTRAINT
92    [FK_Main_Projects] FOREIGN KEY([ProjectID])
93  REFERENCES [dbo].[Projects] ([ProjectID])
94
95  ALTER TABLE [dbo].[Main] CHECK CONSTRAINT [FK_Main_Projects]
96
97  ALTER TABLE [dbo].[MyProjects]  WITH NOCHECK ADD  CONSTRAINT
```

```
 98    [FK_MyProjects_Employees] FOREIGN KEY([EmployeeID])
 99  REFERENCES [dbo].[Employees] ([EmployeeID])
100  NOT FOR REPLICATION
101
102  ALTER TABLE [dbo].[MyProjects] NOCHECK CONSTRAINT
103    [FK_MyProjects_Employees]
104
105  -- Note the CASCADE statements
106  ALTER TABLE [dbo].[MyProjects]  WITH CHECK ADD   CONSTRAINT
107    [FK_MyProjects_Projects] FOREIGN KEY([ProjectID])
108  REFERENCES [dbo].[Projects] ([ProjectID])
109  ON DELETE CASCADE
110
111  ALTER TABLE [dbo].[MyProjects] CHECK CONSTRAINT
112    [FK_MyProjects_Projects]
113
114  ALTER TABLE [dbo].[Projects]  WITH CHECK ADD   CONSTRAINT
115   [FK_Projects_Employees] FOREIGN KEY([ManagerID])
116  REFERENCES [dbo].[Employees] ([EmployeeID])
117  ON UPDATE SET NULL
118  ON DELETE SET NULL
119
120  ALTER TABLE [dbo].[Projects] CHECK CONSTRAINT
121   [FK_Projects_Employees]
```

3.5   TimeReg Data sample

For use in SQL experiments, screen dumps etc. we need neutral project
data. A part of the design is that we have projects that may have child-
projects. Data can be accumulated on the parent when presenting to
management, whereas they can be used inside the project on a more de-
tailed level. In B&K Denmark we use these children for subteams like
FPGA, Embedded Software etc. while another country use the children for
various phases in a project.

In the sample for this book the parent projects are named after the planets
in our solar-system. The children of the planets are named after their
moons - although far from all moons are included. In the Projects table
there is a "Parent" column[2]. This contains the ProjectID of the parent
project. For the parent projects, the value in this column is 0. Projects
such as "Vacation" and "Sickness" are special since some privacy may be
needed. For these the Parent is -1. In Chapter 4 a SELECT is done that
shows the projects in Table 4.2.

---

[2]A more consistent name would have been "ParentID"

Chapter 4

SQL

4.1 Introduction to SQL

Typically, when people talk about SQL-statements they mean queries like the SELECT that we have already seen in some examples when discussing JOIN. SELECT together with UPDATE, DELETE and INSERT constitutes the "data manipulation language".

We have seen them bundled together as CRUD in Chapter 2. We have also seen some commands used for creating and deleting tables and databases - like CREATE, ALTER and DROP. This is the "data definition language". These two groups of commands are the most important in this book, but altogether there are four groups - as shown in Table 4.1.

Table 4.1: T-SQL Language Groups

Term	Meaning	Examples
DML	Data manipulation language	SELECT, UPDATE, DELETE, INSERT
DDL	Data definition language	ALTER, CREATE, DROP
DCL	Data control language	GRANT, REVOKE
TCL	Transactional control language	COMMIT, ROLLBACK

You can find a lot of details on SQL and T-SQL on the internet. One of the best places is "w3schools.com". This shows all the generic SQL commands as well as specific T-SQL for SQL Server. In this text we will walk through some samples, to get a general understanding.

4.1.1   Parameters

The samples are taken from the database-interface layer that we will dig further into in Chapter 7. Here all SQL-statements are built as C# strings. I have removed the C# string stuff in the following listings to focus on the T-SQL. However, I have kept the "parameters". These are variable names that start with a "@". We shall see later that these parameters are not substituted in the C#-string before it is handed to SQL server. Instead the parameters are handed over separately in a *Command* object. This improves security - especially when strings originate directly from the user. In such a case, a bandit could supply a full nasty SQL statement instead of just a name or similar - the so-called SQL-injection. This is not possible with parameters. It is important to show this syntax to get used to using parameters. As a bonus it also makes it clearer which part of the SQL that is input from the application. Note that it is perfectly legal to use names for parameters that are identical to the relevant column-names.

Another name for the use of parameters is *binding*. Whenever SQL Server receives an SQL-statement it is "compiled" into an *execution plan*. This is cached, and if SQL Server later runs into the same SQL Statement, it will reuse the execution plan. Thus performance is boosted. However, the textual SQL statement must be exactly the same, whereas parameters may differ without triggering a new execution plan. Naturally, parameters are typically where changes are likely found, so binding, or using parameters, can greatly enhance performance. We will get back to execution plans when we discuss *indexes*.

4.1.2   SELECT

Listing 4.1 is a simple SELECT that should return exactly one row from the "Projects" table, and only the "Name" column from this. The limiting factor is the *WHERE* clause which filters the answer and only gives us rows that match the expression. WHERE can - and typically should - also be used in UPDATE and DELETE.

Listing 4.1: Simple Select

```
1  SELECT Name
2  FROM Projects
3  WHERE ProjectID = @ProjectID
```

There should never be more than one row in the result of this query as we are filtering with a primary key. We expect more than zero rows as we are using a key from an earlier result. But what if the project has been deleted? Wouldn't that mean that 0 rows are returned? Yes, but in this application, projects are normally not deleted - only closed for further entries. Otherwise hours would get "lost".

As stated, projects are not deleted, but nevertheless there are not that many of them. So, instead of querying for individual pieces of information on single projects like in Listing 4.1, it makes mores sense to fill a C# dictionary for general lookup when the application is initialized. The T-SQL for this is shown in Listing 4.2. This time all projects are needed - so no WHERE clause.

Listing 4.2: Select with Joins

```
1  SELECT P1.ProjectID, P1.Name, P1.Parent,
2      P2.Name As ParentName, E.FullName
3  FROM Projects AS P1
4      LEFT JOIN Projects AS P2
5          ON P1.Parent = P2.ProjectID
6      LEFT JOIN Employees AS E
7          ON P1.ManagerID = E.EmployeeID
```

Now we have two left joins, "extending" the rows of the Projects table. First it is extended with itself. This is because projects can have parent projects (but not grandparents). To find these, we join on ProjectID - the primary key - and Parent - technically a "foreign key". Finally, we join with the Employees table. The Projects table only contain the foreign key to the EmployeeID, and to get the managers name, we need to join with the Employees table.

Table 4.2 shows a sample output when running the SQL from Listing 4.2.

Table 4.2: Projects with Parents

ProjectID	Name	Parent	ParentName	FullName
1	Vacation	-1	NULL	NULL
2	Sickness	-1	NULL	NULL
3	Venus	0	NULL	Klaus Elk
4	Mercury	0	NULL	Klaus Elk
5	Earth	0	NULL	Klaus Elk
6	Mars	0	NULL	Klaus Elk
7	Jupiter	0	NULL	Peter Nielsen
8	Saturn	0	NULL	Klaus Elk
9	Uranus	0	NULL	Klaus Elk
10	Neptune	0	NULL	Klaus Elk
11	Phobos	6	Mars	Klaus Elk
12	Deimos	6	Mars	Klaus Elk
13	Moon	5	Earth	Klaus Elk
14	Titan	8	Saturn	Klaus Elk
15	Enceladus	8	Saturn	Klaus Elk
16	Io	7	Jupiter	Peter Nielsen
17	Europe	7	Jupiter	Peter Nielsen

4.1.3 INSERT, UPDATE and DELETE

Listing 4.3 shows a typical INSERT. In TimeReg, rows are inserted one per SQL-command only. It *is* possible to do an insert with several rows at the same time. However, the code is more clean when only single rows are inserted - possibly inside a loop. The downside is that this causes more trips to the database. The upside is that we will reuse an execution plan.

There are no primary keys in the relevant table - MyProjects. It is an association - or junction - table with pairs of foreign keys. As stated earlier, it is created with a constraint - assuring that there is max 1 row with a given ProjectID *and* EmployeeID. Thus, this action might cause an error - an exception in C#.

Listing 4.4 shows the corresponding DELETE. Note that again we see the WHERE clause. In this case it is very important. Without the WHERE, the statement will delete *all* rows.

Listing 4.3: Simple Insert

```
1  INSERT INTO MyProjects (ProjectID, EmployeeID)
2  VALUES (@ProjectID, @EmployeeID)
```

Listing 4.4: Simple Delete

```
1  DELETE FROM MyProjects
2  WHERE ProjectID = @ProjectID
3     AND EmployeeID = @EmployeeID
```

Listing 4.5 shows an update of an existing row. Again we see the very important WHERE clause.

Listing 4.5: Simple Update

```
1  UPDATE Projects
2  SET Name = @Name, ProjectNo = @ProjectNo , PSONumber = @PSONumber ,
3     Category = @Category , Grouptag = @Grouptag
4  WHERE ProjectID = @ProjectID
```

A good trick when doing DELETEs and UPDATEs, is to start by creating a similar SELECT to test the WHERE part. When this returns all the relevant rows - and only these - you can substitute the SELECT with the relevant command. Still you might want to test on a non-production version as well.

4.2 Next Level SQL

In the following we will look at some more advanced T-SQL.

4.2.1 Identity

When discussing keys in Chapter 2, I recommended the use of surrogate keys - especially the "identity" running-number generated by SQL Server. Often, when a row has been inserted and such a key created, you want to know it in your code. One reason is that it might be needed right away as a foreign key in another table. You could query for it, but this means yet a visit to the database and without the key that you need, it becomes a "catch 22". Much more efficient to get the key right away. This is demonstrated in Listing 4.6.

Listing 4.6: Insert with new Identity

```
1  INSERT INTO Main (EmployeeID, Date, ProjectID, Hours, Comment)
2  OUTPUT INSERTED.MainID
3  VALUES (@EmployeeID, @Date, @ProjectID, @Hours, @Comment)
```

4.2.2   Group By

A report is needed that per employee states the projects that this person
has worked on with monthly sums. The solution is found in Listing 4.7. By
using the T-SQL "SUM" command, a new virtual column is created - here
conveniently named "Total". The ROUND-function rounds the number
to an integer. The YEAR and MONTH - together with the "GROUP BY" -
organizes the sums into *amortized* values - sums per month per year. There
is no guarantee that all this comes out in the right order. This is why there
is also an ORDER BY.

All this may look a little complex, but it is actually not so difficult to write.
However, you get incredibly much value for the few lines of code. The
speed with which SQL Server travels through all these data and sends back
amortized numbers is amazing.

Listing 4.7: Amortized Sums

```
1  SELECT Employees.FullName, Employees.Department, projects.ProjectID,
2     YEAR(main.Date) AS Year, MONTH(main.Date) AS Month,
3     ROUND(SUM(main.Hours),0) as Total
4  FROM PROJECTS projects
5     INNER JOIN Main main
6        ON main.ProjectID = projects.ProjectID
7     INNER JOIN Employees
8        ON main.EmployeeID = Employees.EmployeeID
9  WHERE main.Date >= @FromDate AND main.Date <= @ToDate
10 GROUP BY Employees.FullName, Employees.Department, projects.ProjectID,
11     Year(main.Date), Month(main.Date)
12 ORDER BY Employees.FullName, projects.ProjectID,
13     Year(main.Date), Month(main.Date)
```

Note that Listing 4.7 only joins with the Employees table - not with the
Projects table. Thus, the result contains names of people but only IDs
of Projects. When project info is needed in the application, ProjectID is
used as a key into the Projects dictionary. See the resulting output in Table
4.3 which contains 3 months for two employees. Note how the output is
grouped and sorted. "John Hansen" comes before "Klaus Elk" because

employees are sorted by their full name, whereas projects are sorted by their "ProjectID".

Looking at the output, it is also clear that grouping on department really makes no sense as this follows the employee. However, if this is removed from the "GROUP BY", we get the following error-message: *"Column 'Employees.Department' is invalid in the select list because it is not contained in either an aggregate function or the GROUP BY clause."* Based on this, a simple solution is to include Department in the GROUP BY as shown.

Also note that the "Month" column skips months where the Total is 0. This can cause problems in a program looping through data.

Table 4.3: Orders

FullName	Department	ProjectID	Year	Month	Total
John Hansen	75	1	2018	2	24
John Hansen	75	1	2018	3	16
John Hansen	75	2	2018	3	40
John Hansen	75	4	2018	1	16
John Hansen	75	4	2018	2	40
John Hansen	75	4	2018	3	54
John Hansen	75	9	2018	1	52
John Hansen	75	9	2018	2	48
John Hansen	75	9	2018	3	40
John Hansen	75	10	2018	1	40
John Hansen	75	11	2018	1	56
John Hansen	75	11	2018	2	40
John Hansen	75	15	2018	1	12
John Hansen	75	15	2018	2	8
John Hansen	75	15	2018	3	10
Klaus Elk	75	1	2018	2	40
Klaus Elk	75	1	2018	3	32
Klaus Elk	75	2	2018	1	16
Klaus Elk	75	6	2018	1	48
Klaus Elk	75	6	2018	2	5
Klaus Elk	75	6	2018	3	35
Klaus Elk	75	7	2018	1	44
Klaus Elk	75	7	2018	2	35
Klaus Elk	75	7	2018	3	24
Klaus Elk	75	8	2018	1	6
Klaus Elk	75	8	2018	2	16
Klaus Elk	75	8	2018	3	18
Klaus Elk	75	11	2018	1	30
Klaus Elk	75	11	2018	2	26
Klaus Elk	75	11	2018	3	32
Klaus Elk	75	15	2018	1	40
Klaus Elk	75	15	2018	2	37
Klaus Elk	75	15	2018	3	22

4.3   Learnings on CRUD

From the few examples we can deduce a number of rules of thumb:

❑ SELECT statements can become quite complex, especially when reports with aggregated numbers are needed. This is in line with the discussion on OLTP versus OLAP. This database is not tailored specifically towards historical analysis, so when this is needed, things become more complex.

❑ DELETE, UPDATE and INSERT typically are rather simple. This is what the OLTP system excels in.

❑ Where a SELECT may return thousands of rows, the DELETE, UPDATE and INSERT typically only operate on a single row. Once in a while you may need to do some maintenance - in our sample it could be to move hours from one project to another. In such a case UPDATE is typically used on several rows. The same could happen with DELETE, but rarely with INSERT.

❑ The WHERE clause must not be forgotten in DELETE and UPDATE - without this all existing rows are affected.

❑ Use **OUTPUT** `Inserted.<ColumnName>` to get an updated identity value.

4.4   Indexing

Indexes are generally extra tables created for faster searches - and thereby improved performance. As stated earlier: SQL Server does an OK job on indexes right out of the box. Basically it simply creates indexes for the primary keys. This makes sense as these are used in joins. When you create a unique constraint - as we have seen earlier - it also creates an index for the relevant columns. That's it. In many scenarios that's fine.

A table can have many indexes, but only one can be *clustered*. A clustered index organizes the actual table according to the column(s) selected for the index. The logical consequence is that all other indexes are non-clustered.

It is possible to overdo indexing. Small tables are faster without index. Any change in a table (UPDATE, INSERT or DELETE) requires an update of the relevant indexes. SQL Server utilizes its indexes and look-ups best when many rows are addressed by the same SQL-statement. Thus indexes really shine when it comes to large tables, mainly used in SELECT. When deciding which columns to index, a good place to start is to look at the WHERE statements in your queries. Columns used in comparisons here are good candidates.

For the TimeReg application I want the daily INSERTs and UPDATEs for the developers to be fast, in order not to demotivate them. On the other hand - managers with their queries will wait. These queries are rarer, and more rewarding. The conclusion seems to be: no extra indexes.

However, all employee updates start with the SELECT of the current week. This is data for a given employee and for a specific range of dates (a week)[1], so would it make sense to create an index based on these?

Let us test Management Studio's very nice display of the *execution plan*. As described earlier, when SQL Server receives a new query it "compiles" it into an execution plan.

When a query is visible you can press CTRL-M or select "Query" in the main menu, then "Include Actual Execution Plan". Then press F5 to run the query.

Now a third output tab appears after "Results" and "Messages", named "Execution Plan". This is shown in Figure 4.1. Let's take a look at the query in the top window.

The query starts with CHECKPOINT and DROPCLEANBUFFERS. Together these assure that the query starts from a clean sheet with nothing clever in memory from the previous run - e.g. "compiled" SQL statements. After these commands we see:

SET STATISTICS **TIME ON** and
SET STATISTICS IO **ON.**

---

[1]Whether the BETWEEN command is used for a range, or two comparisons, makes no difference.

After the query these are set to OFF to minimize the output in the Messages window for the start of next round:

```
DBCC execution completed. If DBCC printed error messages,
contact your system administrator.

 SQL Server Execution Times:
   CPU time = 0 ms,  elapsed time = 0 ms.

(17 row(s) affected)
Table 'Projects'. Scan count 0, logical reads 34, physical reads 2,
read-ahead reads 0, lob logical reads 0, lob physical reads 0,
lob read-ahead reads 0.
Table 'Worktable'. Scan count 0, logical reads 0, physical reads 0,
read-ahead reads 0, lob logical reads 0, lob physical reads 0,
lob read-ahead reads 0.
Table 'Main'. Scan count 1, logical reads 855, physical reads 3,
read-ahead reads 851, lob logical reads 0, lob physical reads 0,
lob read-ahead reads 0.

(1 row(s) affected)

 SQL Server Execution Times:
   CPU time = 31 ms,  elapsed time = 210 ms.
```

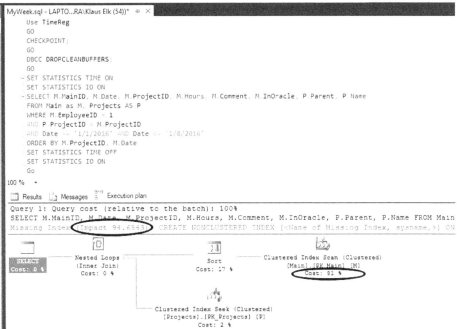

Figure 4.1: Execution plan without index

We see that the query uses 31 ms of CPU-time. This deviates from one run to another but stays in this area. The *Worktable* mentioned here is a temporary object created by SQL Server. For this exercise we focus on the "Main" table. The *logical reads* are reads from memory cache, while *physical reads* are from disc. If we look at the execution plan we get all kinds of advanced information by hovering the mouse over the relevant part of the execution. We see that 81% of the time is spent on a clustered *Index Scan*. A scan means going through the whole table.

We also see a (green) text: "Missing Index (Impact 94.6543)". This means that we may save 95% of the execution time with the right index. If we right-click and select "Missing Index Details" we get a new query window - see Listing 4.8.

Listing 4.8: Index Suggestion

```
1  /*
2  Missing Index Details from MyWeek.sql
3  The Query Processor estimates that implementing the
4  following index could improve the query cost by 94.6543%.
5  */
6
7  /*
8  USE [TimeReg]
9  GO
10 CREATE NONCLUSTERED INDEX [<Name of Missing Index, sysname,>]
11 ON [dbo].[Main] ([EmployeeID],[Date])
12 INCLUDE ([MainID],[ProjectID],[Hours],[Comment],[InOracle])
13 GO
14 */
```

Lines 10-12 in the Listing is an instruction to build an index on EmployeeID and Date - just as expected. We uncomment the code and replace "[<Name of Missing Index, sysname,>]" with "[IX_Employee_Date]", and press F5.

The top window is the same query, but the new bottom window is now seen in Figure 4.2. The Index Scan has become an *Index Seek* in our non-clustered IX_Employee_Date. This is now 10% - and thus not the bottleneck anymore. The other index seek that was 2% before is now 54 %. Naturally the absolute timing of the latter seek is unchanged, it's just a larger proportion of the total.

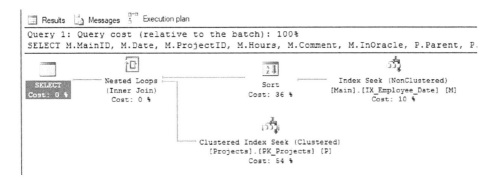

Figure 4.2: Execution plan with index

The "Messages" window now says:

```
DBCC execution completed. If DBCC printed error messages, contact your system
administrator.

 SQL Server Execution Times:
   CPU time = 0 ms,  elapsed time = 0 ms.

(17 row(s) affected)
Table 'Projects'. Scan count 0, logical reads 34, physical reads 2,
read-ahead reads 0, lob logical reads 0, lob physical reads 0,
lob read-ahead reads 0.
Table 'Worktable'. Scan count 0, logical reads 0, physical reads 0,
read-ahead reads 0, lob logical reads 0, lob physical reads 0,
lob read-ahead reads 0.
Table 'Main'. Scan count 1, logical reads 3, physical reads 3,
read-ahead reads 0, lob logical reads 0, lob physical reads 0,
lob read-ahead reads 0.

(1 row(s) affected)

 SQL Server Execution Times:
   CPU time = 0 ms,  elapsed time = 338 ms.
```

CPU time is now 0 ms (rounded). The I/O explains why.

Relatively this index was a big success. Whether it makes sense to go for 32 ms is another thing. Network delays can easily be much longer.

4.5   Views

A database-manager can choose to only make certain columns of a table accessible for (some) users, by creating a *view* of the table with only the selected columns - and even rename some or all. Programmers work on the table via the view, and may think of it as just another table. This is one way to use views, where the purpose is limited access or better naming without disturbing backward compatibility.

Another reason for creating views is to simplify the client programs. Advanced joins can be written as part of SQL-code embedded in your program. Alternatively a view can be created in the database environment. This makes all client programs simpler, as they just need to refer to the view in the same way as to a table. In reality the view is dynamically generated when data is requested.

If a view is based on a single table, it is possible to insert, update and delete rows, as if it really *is* a table, and the underlying, real table will be updated correctly. If however, the view is dynamically created from a join, you cannot simply write to the view and have the underlying tables updated. This requires the use of something called "Instead of" *triggers* that is beyond the scope of this book.

After having run TimeReg for some time with a growing user-base and new requirements in small doses, we were faced with a completely new requirement: forecasts. In addition to registering hours, managers would estimate man-months per man per month per project.

The Forecasts table was created in Management Studio, using the Designer. Using "Script Table as..." now gives us Listing 4.9.

Listing 4.9: Forecast table

```
1  CREATE TABLE [dbo].[Forecasts](
2          [TaskID]      [int] IDENTITY(1,1)  NOT NULL,
3          [ProjectID]   [int]                NOT NULL,
4          [EmployeeID]  [int]                NOT NULL,
5          [TaskDescr]   [varchar](200)       NOT NULL,
6          [CalMonth]    [int]                NOT NULL,
7          [Effort]      [real]               NOT NULL,
8  PRIMARY KEY CLUSTERED
9  (
10         [TaskID] ASC
11 )...
```

We recognize the use of an integer surrogate key - here named "TaskID". EmployeeID and ProjectID are well-known by now, and "TaskDescr" is a textual description of the job to do. "Effort" is the number of months a developer is estimated to put in a task in the given month. Thus, it should be a number between 0 and 1, but could be more if we start thinking in competence pools - like e.g. "DSP Developers".

Instead of the high-resolution time-stamps an integer is used. This is called "CalMonth" and is created like: Year*100+Month, so that February 2018 becomes 201802. Table 4.4 shows the first 10 lines of forecasts in this system[2].

Table 4.4: Forecast - first 10 lines

TaskID	ProjID	EmplID	TaskDescr	CalMonth	Effort
6	275	18	Basic Linux	201612	1
19	275	215	Basic Linux	201612	1
32	275	5	Basic Linux	201612	1
63	73	121	FPGA Design	201610	1
64	73	121	FPGA Design	201611	0.7
65	73	121	FPGA Impl	201612	0.7
66	73	121	FPGA Impl	201701	0.7
67	73	121	FPGA Impl	201702	1
68	73	121	FPGA Test	201703	1
69	73	121	FPGA Test	201704	1

After the forecasts were created we wanted to show them in *Power BI*. The custom date-format was not compatible with this tool. In order to give Power BI the ability to read time-stamps "normally", a view was created. This is also done in Management Studio, by right-clicking on "Views". You get to a dialog where you can pick tables and columns in these. This gives you some SQL that you can edit. It is not difficult to write the script directly. The final script is seen in Listing 4.10.

Finally, Table 4.5 shows the first 10 lines of a SELECT * on this view[3]. It is easy to see the effect of the view. Please note that it is not possible to write to this view to get data into the Forecast table. This is not relevant

---

[2]Headernames shortened to save space

[3]Headernames shortened to save space

Listing 4.10: Forecast View

```
1  CREATE VIEW [dbo].[ForecastDates] AS
2  SELECT TaskID, ProjectID, EmployeeID, TaskDescr, Effort,
3     DATEFROMPARTS((CalMonth/100),(CALMONTH%100),1) AS TheDate
4  FROM   dbo.Forecasts
5  GO
```

Table 4.5: Forecast - first 10 lines

TaskID	ProjID	EmplID	TaskDescr	Effort	TheDate
6	275	18	Basic Linux	1	2016-12-01
19	275	215	Basic Linux	1	2016-12-01
32	275	5	Basic Linux	1	2016-12-01
63	73	121	FPGA Design	1	2016-10-01
64	73	121	FPGA Design	0.7	2016-11-01
65	73	121	FPGA Impl	0.7	2016-12-01
66	73	121	FPGA Impl	0.7	2017-01-01
67	73	121	FPGA Impl	1	2017-02-01
68	73	121	FPGA Test	1	2017-03-01
69	73	121	FPGA Test	1	2017-04-01

for Power BI anyway. Naturally the view may need to be joined with the Employees and Projects tables.

4.6   Common Table Expressions

It is possible to put queries into queries. These are called *subqueries*. You can also go one step further - to *common table expressions*. This name is often just shortened to *CTE*. A CTE can do whatever a subquery can do, but on top of this it can be recursive. Many believe that CTEs are more readable than subqueries. Thus, we skip subqueries here.

In the first part of the CTE, a temporary named table is created - much like a view. This part starts with "WITH" and the name to use for the temporary table - "CTE" is often used. In the second part of the CTE, the temporary table can be used one or more times - like any other table.

As stated earlier, TimeReg projects can be children of other projects. In the

"Reports" part of TimeReg we need hours from child projects aggregated on the parent - together with hours booked directly on the parent. Listing 4.11 shows the CTE for this (with fixed dates).

Listing 4.11: Common Table Expression

```
1   WITH CTE AS (
2       SELECT Year(main.Date) AS Year, Month(main.Date)
3           AS Month, projects.ProjectID, projects.Parent, main.Hours,
4           CASE WHEN projects.Parent > 0 THEN projects.Parent
5           ELSE projects.ProjectID
6           END SuperProj
7       FROM Projects projects
8           INNER JOIN Main main
9               ON main.ProjectID = projects.ProjectID
10      WHERE main.Date < '2018-4-1' AND main.Date >= '2018-1-1'
11  )
12  SELECT SuperProj, Year, Month, ROUND(SUM(Hours),0) AS Total
13  FROM CTE
14  GROUP BY SuperProj, Year, Month
15  ORDER BY SuperProj, Year, Month
```

In the first part a "SuperProj" column is created in the temporary table. This is the ProjectID of the parent project if such exists. If not, the project is a parent itself.

The first part now continues joining the *actual* project with the Main table to get the hours. Thus, we get all the hours per actual project, but pass them on to the second part together with the SuperProj.

The second part of the CTE starts in line 12. It is responsible for aggregation and grouping/ordering according to the SuperProj, Year and Month. When comparing this to the solution in Subsection 4.2.2, we see that the CTE also gives us fewer columns to worry about when grouping.

The output when executing the code in Listing 4.11 is seen in Table 4.6.

Please note that there are missing entries. E.g. SuperProj 5 has no line for Month 3. SQL Server might have written a total of 0 - but it doesn't. This can be a nasty surprise to a programmer using these data to fill out arrays or writing in monthly columns.

Table 4.6: CTE with SuperProj aggregated hours

SuperProj	Year	Month	Total
1	2018	1	24
1	2018	2	104
1	2018	3	104
2	2018	1	16
2	2018	2	40
2	2018	3	40
4	2018	1	16
4	2018	2	40
4	2018	3	54
5	2018	1	32
5	2018	2	60
6	2018	1	134
6	2018	2	71
6	2018	3	67
7	2018	1	124
7	2018	2	55
7	2018	3	98
8	2018	1	106
8	2018	2	61
8	2018	3	80
9	2018	1	52
9	2018	2	48
9	2018	3	40
10	2018	1	40

4.7 Stored Procedures

A stored procedure is basically a query where the SQL-text is not part of the client program, but instead is stored in SQL Server, together with the database and views etc. We see later how ADO.net attaches the SQL-text, and parameters to this, as separate objects in the *SqlCommand*. When using a stored procedure, we still attach the parameters, but instead of attaching the SQL text, we name the stored procedure to use.

Performance-wise this is a bit faster, since the query already is "compiled" into an execution plan. If several clients are to use the same database, we can put SQL into stored procedures, and thus don't need to write the same code several times. It may also be a good way to split the work in a team.

There are however, syntactical differences, and it *is* yet a thing to learn. This book is about SQL Server and C#, and we will not go further into stored procedures.

4.8 Security and Connection Strings

For many years the way to setup a connection to a database has involved a *connection string*. Probably because this is more language independent than e.g. a structure. Here is an example:

```
private static string TestLocalConnectionStr =
"Data Source=localhost\\sqlexpress;Initial Catalog=TimeReg;
Integrated Security=True";
```

This string contains three "value-pairs" - separated by ";":

❐ **Data Source = XXX**
The "Data Source" is the server to connect to. In the example a server named "sqlexpress" on "localhost" (this PC) is used. This is the default name for an SQL Express installation.

❐ **Initial Catalog = YYY**
The "Catalog" is the name of the database on the server selected

above. In the example it is called "TimeReg".

☐ **Integrated Security = ZZZ**
When the "Integrated Security" parameter is set to "True", the connection uses *Windows Authentication*. Thus, if the user has read and write access rights on the given Server+Catalog, he or she can use any of the CRUD commands. If the "Integrated Security" is set to False, the string must contain another way to authenticate. Integrated Security is generally considered the safest choice.

The above three parameters are a "minimal set" - there are many others.

As stated, the use of a connection string is the traditional way, but it is actually possible to work with structures, using *SqlConnectionStringBuilder*. With this we can get/set value-pairs with a classic "member" syntax like in lines 3+4 in Listing 4.12. Alternatively we can use indexers - as in lines 6+7.

Listing 4.12: SqlConnectionStringBuilder

```
1  SqlConnectionStringBuilder builder =
2              new SqlConnectionStringBuilder(GetConnectionString());
3  builder.Password = "CrispyChip";
4  builder.AsynchronousProcessing = true;
5
6  builder["Connect_Timeout"] = 2000;
7  builder["Trusted_Connection"] = true;
```

In the connection-string we use integrated security. Alternatively we might write `User ID=TimeRegUser; Password=myPassword`. This is e.g. used with *SQL Server authentication*.

Figures 4.3 and 4.4 shows how a user is created using Management Studio.

① In the Object Explorer there is a "Security" node on the same level as the databases. As the figure shows, there is also a "Security" node under each database. Click to expand the tree below the outer Security node.

② Right click on "Logins" sub-node and select "New Login ..." to get to the dialog in the figure. Note that the default choice here is Windows authentication, which is the same as Integrated Security. If we want this, we can simply type or paste the username[4] in here, or open the search dialog to find this user. We could also select a group of users from an organization's "Active Directory". With Integrated Security we do not need to come up with passwords, as we use the users normal passwords. In Figure 4.3 "SQL Server authentication" is selected.

③ This step is only valid when using SQL Server authentication. In the "General" page, create the user with a relevant password. Here the name is "TimeRegUser" - also shown in Figure 4.3. This allows the user access to the RDBMS - but there is no connection to any specific database(s) - yet.

④ This step is the same for SQL Server authentication and Integrated Security. We now have a legal user that may log in to the server. But the server alone is not interesting. In the "User Mapping" page, select the relevant database (here "TimeReg"), and assign the relevant roles. Figure 4.4 shows check-marks for `db_datareader` and `db_datawriter`. Click on the ellipsis (...) button in the "Default Schema" column to open a dialog, where relevant schemas can be browsed. Select the relevant one - in this case the default "dbo".

⑤ The SQL Server authenticated user "TimeRegReader" may now be created similarly - but only with `db_datareader`. This is handy for allowing a wider access with 3'rd party tools for pure analysis.

⑥ After the above, the new user is also found under the relevant database's "Security/Users".

If SQL Server authentication is used, anyone can log into the database as long as they provide the right username and password in the connection string. The obvious downside is that the string is written in clear text. This makes it visible for anyone who has access to the source code (problematic) or uses e.g. *ILDASM* on the "executable" (worse) or uses *WireShark* on key points in the network (also bad).

Listing 4.13 was created by applying Microsofts .net-tool ILDASM on TimeReg.exe, then selecting "DBUtil" - the database layer - and then clicking on the constructor - "ctor". Note that the password is easily found to be "TimeIsOnMySide".

---

[4]This is given as $< Domain/Workgroup > \backslash < UserName >$

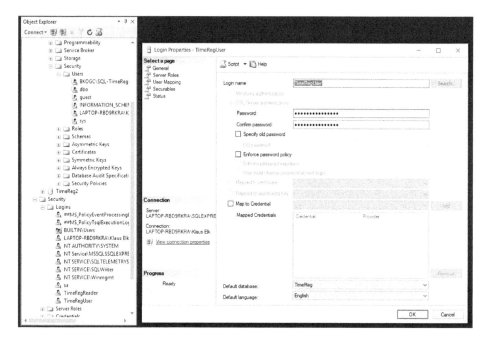

Figure 4.3: Setup of a SQL Server user with password

Listing 4.13: ILDasm on TimeReg

```
1        void   .cctor() cil managed
2  {
3  // Code size       87 (0x57)
4  .maxstack  1
5  IL_0000: ldstr    "Data_Source=localhost\\sqlexpress;Initial_Catalog=T"
6  + "imeReg;Persist_Security_Info=False;User_ID=TimeRegUser;Password=TimeI"
7  + "sOnMySide"
8  .....
```

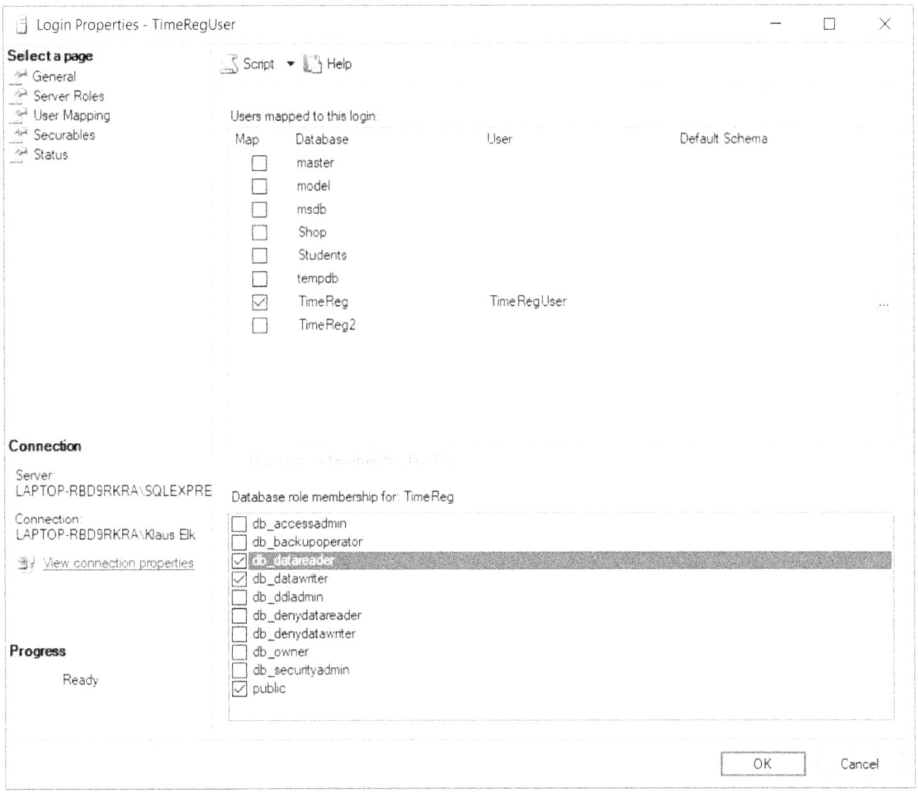

Figure 4.4: Assign access rights to TimeReg database

It is possible to get around the clear-text problem by using encrypted values from e.g. web.config (ASP.net) or app.config (Windows Forms) files. This is however outside the scope of this book.

Part II

C# Programming

Chapter 5

Overall Design

5.1 Database Frameworks

Between the object-oriented world and the relational database world there are some inherent clashes:

OBJECT ORIENTATION FAVORS INFORMATION HIDING AND ENCAPSULATION. DATABASES ARE ALL ABOUT EXPOSING DATA.

As described in subsection 2.5.4 there are also very different ways to handle containment - collections versus relations. Finally, the data-types in the database and the object-oriented programming-language are typically not the same. On top of all this, SQL may not be the programmers favorite language. These are some reasons why various frameworks may seem appealing.

Is there a way to use a database without losing focus on the application at hand? Figure 5.1 shows the major choices of frameworks for developing database applications with Visual Studio. The frameworks are the gray boxes between the C# application and *ADO.net*. Thus, ADO.net is the foundation for all the frameworks, but it can also be used directly from application code. ADO.net directly interfaces to SQL Server and via older technologies such as ODBC and OLE DB to Excel, XML, Sharepoint and other SQL-databases.

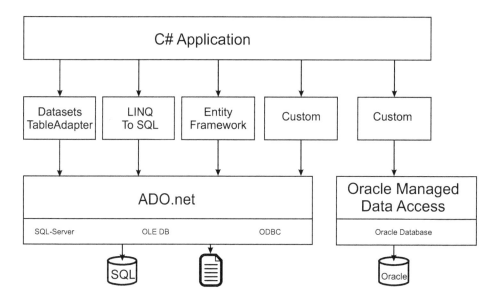

Figure 5.1: Various Database Frameworks

The figure also includes *Oracle Managed Data Access*, since this is created in such a way that it looks pretty much like ADO.net. In this way you can use Oracle through one of the frameworks and ADO.net, or you can use it more directly via Oracles pendant to ADO.net - Oracle Managed Data Access. We will look more closely into this in Section 7.6.

As mentioned in Subsection 2.5.6, I once developed a database for maintaining components for an Altium CAD system. The database was created in Management Studio and imported into Visual Studio, which generated a number of *TableAdapters* for *Datasets* - the leftmost framework in Figure 5.1. The outcome is shown in Figure 5.2 (low quality).

It really was a quick way to get started, but soon became very frustrating. There is a saying: "crossing the river to get water". That was how it felt. Every little change was buried deep in a dialog - or maybe even had to be written into the generated code. Even when a solution to a problem was found earlier, I had a hard time finding it again whenever I wanted to reuse it. It was not fun, and I decided that I would not get into this again. As we will see later, in Section 7.5, ADO.net actually has its own powerful "adapter" named *SqlDataAdapter*, working with a so-called *DataSet*. This is easy overlooked in all the noise about frameworks and especially the TableAdapters due to the naming similarity.

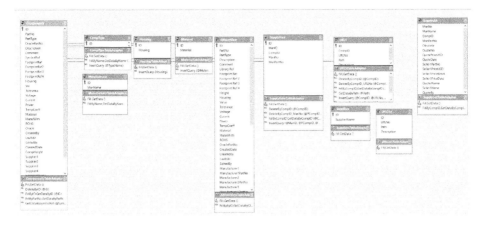

Figure 5.2: Component Database TableAdapters

Even though "Entity Framework" is now recommended by Microsoft, and probably better than the TableAdapters, it is not known for its speed and easy customization.

With Microsoft new fancy stuff quickly can become old "legacy" stuff. This seems to have happened with "Linq-To-SQL" which was very hot for a few years. Whenever this happens you are probably better off with custom standard-based code than with some abandoned wizardry. I do use Linq, but only for the extension-classes that makes it easier to work with collections using "lampda expressions".

In reality ADO.net is a very nice framework by itself. Microsoft refers to it as *Middleware*. Contrary to the many frameworks on top of ADO.net, it has been present and useful since .net version 1.0. To a large degree it existed even before .net. ADO originally meant ActiveX Data Objects. ActiveX is the technology generation before .net - also known as COM. Some basic concepts have survived all the way. Twenty years ago I worked with the old ADO. Even then it had *Connection* and *Command* objects etc.

I recommend a custom "tailored" interface based on ADO.net, following a few simple patterns. These patterns are used with TimeReg. They were directly reusable when making a similar interface to Oracle.

We will go into details with the custom interface library/layer in this book. The patterns basically originate from various application notes and a few personal inventions. Thus, the layer is on one hand tailored to the specific purpose, but on the other hand based on patterns that are easily reused. Extending the database with new tables and queries is now a routine exercise.

5.2   Layers and State

One of the major challenges in program-design is to create the right number of layers. With too few layers the code gets messy. With too many layers you go through a lot of motions that mostly only generate heat. It sometimes feels as if the more layers you put in - the more advanced and fancy is the design. Of course that's not the case.

There are many different patterns - Model-View-Control, Model-View-Presenter, Model-View-Model etc. TimeReg is a small one-man project, and I decided that for the UI-part I would simply "go with the flow" and create simple forms the way Visual Studio facilitates them. This means one class per dialog/screen. I used a simple and classic Windows Forms-based approach. I did make a fully functional version on WPF - Windows Presentation Foundation - but I felt that I lost control and dropped it. You may prefer WPF, and you will still be able to use 99% of the patterns in this book.

The major downside of this simple design is that there is no easy way to do automated testing. Some of the patterns mentioned above allows test-scripts to "fake it" as real users - bypassing only a thin UI-layer. In this project all tests were manual - performed on a local SQL Express installation. Regular backups from the production server were restored onto this server for tests.

A completely different alternative to Forms and WPF is to create a web-based solution based on ASP - Active Server Pages. This is closer to WPF with its "code behind". You can also say that it's just another way of Model-View-Control. I have not tried an ASP-version of TimeReg - yet.

With the application being so database-centric, it was clear that a layer was needed that would handle - and isolate - all the database-interactions. As previously described, this was not to be a standard Microsoft framework. I ended with one "library" for interfacing with SQL Server called "DBUtil", and another one for the Oracle export. As this book is about SQL Server, we will focus on the first, and show a sample from the latter.

The UI-layer has classes that are instantiated with the given dialog, and left for garbage-collection when the dialog is closed. Thus, they only carry *transient state*. The same goes for the DBUtil layer, which mainly serves as a function library. It is used for fetching or storing data in the database, but in-between these calls it does not keep state. The DBUtil-layer does have a number of classes that are instantiated and passed to the caller of the static functions. This is also transient state. This layer gets assistance from ADO.net - handling connection-state and even pooling connections to improve performance.

Why all this talk about state?

IT IS ALWAYS BENEFICIAL TO HAVE A CLEAR IDEA ABOUT WHERE WHICH STATE IS KEPT. IF SEVERAL LAYERS KEEP OVERLAPPING STATE, THERE IS A HUGE RISK THAT THEY ARE GOING TO EVENTUALLY DISAGREE.

Unclear state responsibility leads to all kinds of strange behaviors. Better to keep specific state only one place. In our case the main keeper of state is obviously the database itself - keeping state permanently, even if power is cycled. This is also known as *persistent state*. Finally, there is also state outside the database for the duration of the client application. This is called *application state*.

Clearly, application state must be preserved somewhere: the identity of the current user, the chosen holiday-scheme and whatever settings the user may have. This is kept in the "Model" layer. This Model layer is implemented as a *Singleton* class. A singleton is a class that always is instantiated exactly once. The singleton pattern is practical because it is almost as easy to use from any other class as static functions. You do not need to "carry a data-reference around" - you simply invoke the singleton when needed. The main reason for the "Model" name is that it contains the most complex parts of the *business model*. Table 5.1 is an overview of the layers used in TimeReg - from top to bottom.

Table 5.1: Layers in TimeReg Application - Top-Down

Layer	State	Function
UI	Transient Dialog	Handle the look & feel, logic, menus and events for each form.
Model	Application	User settings and cached collections
DBUtil	Transient	Helper classes for static functions interface between database and collections.
ADO.net	Connection	ADO implements connection pooling and generally keeps state for connections.
Database	Persistent	Stores data from all users - always.

The most important rule when designing and implementing layers is:

ANY LAYER MUST NOT "KNOW" ANYTHING ABOUT ANY LAYERS ABOVE IT.

The database is completely ignorant of the layers above and surely ADO.net knows nothing about our code. This is one of the advantages of using a 3'rd party library. I believe that the rule also applies for the other layers. There is also a secondary rule that says:

IN A *TRULY* LAYERED DESIGN EACH LAYER KNOWS ONLY ABOUT THE LAYER DIRECTLY BENEATH IT.

This rule is hard to live up to, and sure enough: in our sample application the top UI layer knows the Model layer and it knows DBUtil. If this was to be avoided, we would need a lot of functions in the Model layer that more or less copied data between the layer above and beneath. It did not make sense in this scenario. Incidentally - this also applies for the TCP/IP stack where the upper layers know about more than just the layer directly beneath it.

5.3 Class Diagram

Figure 5.3 is an early PowerPoint-drawn UML-diagram of the full TimeReg application. Later a "Forecast" form was added. This is what we will work with in the next chapters. Chapter 6 is all about the model. The following two chapters are dedicated to the DBUtil layer - reflecting the subject for this book. Finally, Chapter 9 covers the forms - focusing on the database interface.

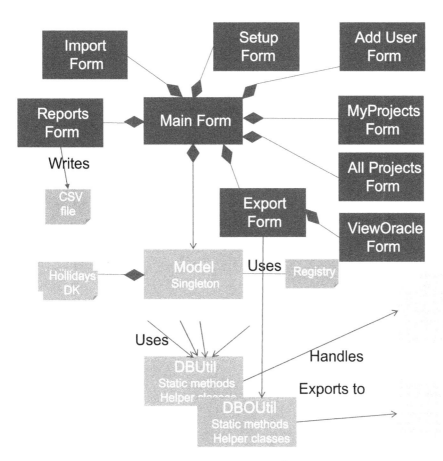

Figure 5.3: UML Diagram - from PowerPoint

Chapter 6

Model Layer

6.1   Initialization

To make life really simple for users, there is no login to the system. When the application is started, the "netname" is read and if the user is found in the database he is "in". If not, he is offered the chance to switch to the right database.

TimeReg started in the danish HQ of Brüel & Kjær. Other departments joined in. There was no real advantage in having all in the same database - so each division got their own base. However, it would not be practical to have different versions of the application.

Each country has their own holiday-calender overlaid onto the weekly timetable. As some departments span several countries, the relevant database and the relevant holidays do not always follow each other.

As stated earlier, the Model layer is where application-state is kept, but where to keep the users choice of database? It does not make sense to have this in the database. Therefore, the choices of database and holiday-scheme are kept in the registry. Listing 6.1 shows how the country-code for the users chosen holiday scheme is read from and written to the database. Note how the *GetValue* method is called with default "DK".

Listing 6.1: Registry access

```
1   private string regKeyName =
2       "Software\\Bruel_and_Kjaer\\TimeReg\\Settings\\";
3   private string regHolidays = "Holidays";
4
5   public string Holidays
6   {
7       get
8       {
9           RegistryKey regKey = Registry.CurrentUser.
10              CreateSubKey(regKeyName);
11          string holidays = regKey.GetValue(
12              regHolidays, "DK").ToString();
13          return holidays;
14      }
15
16      set
17      {
18          RegistryKey regKey = Registry.CurrentUser.
19              CreateSubKey(regKeyName);
20          regKey.SetValue(regHolidays, value);
21      }
22  }
```

Listing 6.2 shows how simple it is to re-initialize the choice of database (catalog) and holidays when the user decides a change - which typically only is done initially and if a new PC is used.

Listing 6.2: Switch base and holidays

```
1   me = System.Environment.UserName.ToLower();
2   //.....
3   public void connect()
4   {
5       string db = (DebugDB) ? "Debug" : Catalog;
6       if (!DBUtil.connect(db))
7           myID = 0;
8       else
9           myID = DBUtil.getEmployeeInfo(me, out superUser, out myFullName);
10
11      if (Holidays.Equals("DK"))
12          setupDKHolidays();
13      else if (Holidays.Equals("UK"))
14          setupUKHolidays();
15      else if (Holidays.Equals("US"))
16          setupUSHolidays();
17      else if (Holidays.Equals("DE"))
18          setupDEHolidays();
19
20      setAccessRights(DBUtil.getAccessRights());
21
22      Dirty = false;
23  }
```

The database choice may be overridden by the "DebugDB" flag which allows the use of a local test database. The code shows my C-heritage: I could have used a switch instead of the if-ladder. Also, there is no default choice here - should an error occur there will simply be no holidays in the calendar.

Based on the netname - "me" - the users ID, name and superuser status are read.

Listing 6.3 shows the 2018 part of the UK holiday list. At the time when this was coded, it made sense to keep this in the application code as a *dictionary*. However, the consequence is that updates to the holiday list requires the application to be updated. It might be more maintenance-friendly to keep the holiday list in the database, where changes can be made easily. The counter-argument is that since holiday-scheme and selected database do not always follow each other, the holiday list would need to be maintained in all databases. So why not in the common application instead?

Listing 6.3: Switch base and holidays

```
1   private void setupUKHolidays()
2   {
3       holidayDict.Add(new DateTime(2018, 1,  1),  "New_Years_Day");
4       holidayDict.Add(new DateTime(2018, 3,  30), "Good_Friday");
5       holidayDict.Add(new DateTime(2018, 4,  2),  "Easter_Monday");
6       holidayDict.Add(new DateTime(2018, 5,  7),  "Early_May_BH");
7       holidayDict.Add(new DateTime(2018, 5,  28), "Spring_BH");
8       holidayDict.Add(new DateTime(2018, 8,  27), "Summer_BH");
9       holidayDict.Add(new DateTime(2018, 12, 25),"Christmas_Day");
10      holidayDict.Add(new DateTime(2018, 12, 26),"Boxing_Day");
11  }
```

Listing 6.4 shows how ISO week numbers are found from the given Monday. United States and Europe do not have the same week-numbers, and C# is not so international in this particular point.

Listing 6.4: Week Number in ISO

```
1   private int curWeekno()
2   {
3       System.Globalization.Calendar cal =
4           System.Globalization.CultureInfo.InvariantCulture.Calendar;
5       // Add 3 days !! - to get the right answer...
6       return cal.GetWeekOfYear(m_monday.AddDays(3),
7       System.Globalization.CalendarWeekRule.
8           FirstFourDayWeek, DayOfWeek.Monday);
9   }
```

Listing 6.5 is something very recently created. More formal requirements
came up as TimeReg was used by more departments. Now, only a few
people should be able to do this, and a few others that. This started as hard-
coded exceptions for specific users, but clearly needed to be maintained in
the database as new people might be assigned roles every now and then,
while others might leave. On the other hand, it would only be a few people,
and only a few checks in the corners of the application. Performance could
never become an issue.

Listing 6.5: Simple Access control

```
 1  public   bool iMayDoThis(string role)
 2  {
 3      string myRoles;
 4      if (m_rolesDict != null && m_rolesDict.TryGetValue(me, out myRoles))
 5      {
 6          myRoles = myRoles.ToLower();
 7          if (myRoles.Contains(role.ToLower()))
 8              return true;
 9      }
10
11      return false;
12  }
```

For this reason, and maybe also as a small rebellion, I decided to make a
table that wasn't even 1NF - see Table 6.1. The first column is the users
netname, and the second column is a space-separated list of roles. This
makes it extremely simple to maintain directly in Management Studio -
saving the time to code an edit-page in TimeReg, while the right to edit
the rights now follow the maintainer of the base. The table is initially read
more or less directly into a dictionary. Whenever the user is e.g. to be
presented with a menu-item, the function "IMayDoThis" returns a boolean
that correspondingly enables or gray's-out the menu-item.

Table 6.1: Non-Normalized Access Rights table

Netname	Roles
jnielsen	Export Projects
kelk	GroupTag ImportUsers AliasSuper DebugDB Projects EditOracle Export
ajones	GroupTag AliasSuper Projects
ajensen	Export
plarsen	Projects Export

6.2   Data for the Main form

The Model deserves its name from the way data from the database is modeled in order to be presented to the user. In most cases, UI *Lists* and *DataGrids* can use functions from DBUtil almost as is - they don't need a pit-stop in the Model layer. There are however exceptions. This is demonstrated in Figure 6.1. To service the main form, a "locallist" is created. This is a shadow structure that contains whatever is needed to provide input to the form - and to get updates back into the database.

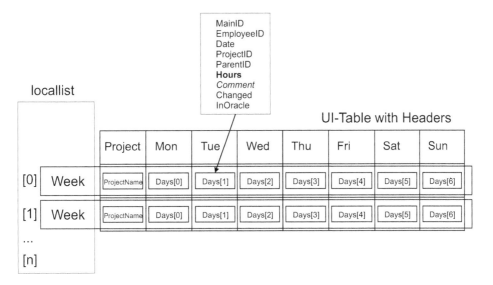

Figure 6.1: Model for main view

Locallist is a list (also usable as array) of object instances of the "Week" class. Each Week instance contains a "ProjectName" and an internal array called "Days", with 7 "CellData" objects. Each CellData instance contains a row from the Main table in the database - joined with Projects and Employees. The basic part is created in DBUtil, and we will get back to this in Chapter 8.

The MainID and other keys are needed when updated data needs to be written back into the database. Cells that are empty before the user starts editing will have a MainID = -1. This means that we will need to *INSERT* data for these. When MainID is >0 we need to *UPDATE* existing rows.

"Hours" is bolded in Figure 6.1 to signify that this is what is used in the cells of the visible UI-table, while "Comment" is in italics because the user will see it as a *datatip* and may choose to edit via a right-click. "Changed" is the only attribute which does not originate from the database. It is a *dirty* flag for the individual cell, telling us whether the user has changed anything.

Handling localList is the most complex process in the basic application[1]. It is divided into the following steps:

① Find the Monday of the week to use. This comes from the "UserView" - the main UI class.

② Retrieve data from the Main table in the database for the given user and week - joined with the relevant project-information. See Listing 6.6. The finer details are done in "DBUtil" which we deal with in Chapter 7.

③ Each row in this joined table now becomes a cell in the "shadow" for a UI table. This is the "localList" described above. It is shown in Figure 6.1.

④ The above only contains projects that already have at least one entry for the selected week. Now add the projects that the user has selected as MyProjects - but not already in the list. These will have all empty cells. This takes place in "addMyProjectsList()" - see Listing 6.7. Note the innocent call to "Sort" at the end of the function. This is only possible because the *interface IComparable* is used in the DBUtil *data-transfer-objects* (more on these later).

⑤ The user updates the UI-table and the localList. This is described in Chapter 9.

⑥ If the user decides to submit the data, all updates, inserts and deletes are handled. This is seen in Listing 6.8

---

[1]Together with Forecasts which we only touch on briefly.

Listing 6.6: Get data for a given Week

```
public List<DBUtil.Week> selectWeekOf(DateTime monday, out int weekno)
{
    m_monday = monday;
    weekno = curWeekno();
    localList = DBUtil.createListFromDB(m_monday, myID);
    addMyProjectsList();
    Dirty = false;
    return localList;
}
```

Listing 6.7: Adding MyProjects

```
public void addMyProjectsList()
{
    DateTime day;
    DBUtil.Week projectWeek = null;
    // We now have a localList with data corresponding
    // to existing projects for this user
    // Now we need to merge in a lot of blanks for the favorites
    // Get the ordered list of project that this user wants to see
    //- also if no data yet
    List<DBUtil.ProjTupple> myprojects = DBUtil.myProjects(myID);

    foreach (DBUtil.ProjTupple myproject in myprojects)
    {
        day = m_monday;
        // Create a weekfull of readonly and "empty" data
        // Add if not already there.
        projectWeek = new DBUtil.Week(myproject.Name);
        // 7 new days of references to CellData
        for (int weekday = 0; weekday < 7; weekday++)
        {
            projectWeek[weekday] = new DBUtil.CellData(
                day.AddDays(weekday),
                myID, myproject.ProjectID, myproject.ParentID);
        }

        if (localList.IndexOf(projectWeek) == -1)
            localList.Add(projectWeek);
    }

    // Now we have got all the stuff in the list
    // and we only need the final step
    localList.Sort();
}
```

Listing 6.8: Update the database

```
 1  public void updateDatabase()
 2  {
 3      // Loop through the rows - each is a project
 4      foreach (DBUtil.Week projectWeek in localList)
 5      {
 6          // Loop through the weekdays of the given project
 7          for (int weekday = 0; weekday < 7; weekday++)
 8          {
 9              if (projectWeek[weekday].Changed)
10              {
11                  if (projectWeek[weekday].MainID == -1)
12                  {
13                      // This is a cell without a database row
14                      // We will not make a new entry with 0.0!
15                      // and yes - you can compare to 0.0F
16                      if (projectWeek[weekday].Hours != 0.0F)
17                          // We need to update the localList mainID;
18                          //if the user makes a new change in the same cell
19                          // it must be an update next time
20                          projectWeek[weekday].MainID =
21                              DBUtil.insertNewMainRow(
22                              projectWeek[weekday].EmployeeID,
23                              projectWeek[weekday].Date,
24                              projectWeek[weekday].ProjectID,
25                              projectWeek[weekday].Hours,
26                              projectWeek[weekday].Comment);
27                  }
28                  else
29                  {
30                      // This is an existing database row
31                      if (projectWeek[weekday].Hours != 0.0F)
32                          DBUtil.updateExistingMainRow(
33                              projectWeek[weekday].MainID,
34                              projectWeek[weekday].Hours,
35                              projectWeek[weekday].Comment);
36                      else
37                          // Inserting a "0" hours now leads
38                          // to a deleted entry
39                          DBUtil.deleteMainRow(
40                              projectWeek[weekday].MainID);
41                  }
42              }
43          }
44      }
45      Dirty = false;
46  }
```

Chapter 7

Database Functions

7.1 Design

The database layer is implemented in a class named "DBUtil". It is a single C#-source file that has two main parts. The first part is the *nested data-heavy classes* that are used to communicate with the upper C# classes. The term "nested" means that they are classes within a class - in this case DBUtil. I use the term "data-heavy" to describe that they are essentially data-carrying and data-exposing classes that are used in the interface to the database. These are also called DTOs - data transfer objects.

The use of public properties with the relevant read/write capabilities make these classes well suited for use in the UI-layer, where they very directly can interface to various lists and particularly a *DataGridView*.

The second part is the actual queries to the database - using the above classes. All these directly database-interfacing functions are static - which is probably not what you would expect. Static functions are super-easy to call, but being static means that you cannot do *multithreading*. There are no local variables per instance. However, they are called synchronously directly from the forms - so they are executed serially. This is a pretty simplistic approach. You may be thinking: "What about worker threads?" or "Why not use async/await?" Microsoft suggests the use of async methods when dealing with databases. However, as stated earlier, I agree with

Einstein: "Keep it as simple as possible - but not simpler".

There are two reasons why this works:

- ❐ The way the workflow is in the application, the user really hasn't got much to do but wait for the database to answer. What is fastest: Waiting synchronously or asynchronously? The asynchronous methods use a lot of energy on setting up and tearing down, while the synchronous methods simply wait. Anyway, the simple queries are pretty fast. Only when we get to the reports does the user sometimes experience a short wait - and again what else is there to do? In the reports the hourglass is turned on before the query and off afterwards, so the user is informed.

- ❐ The functions are static, but they work on the previously described nested data-heavy (DTO) classes which are not static, but are instantiated into objects. These objects *do* have overlapping lifetimes without problems.

7.2   ExecuteNonQuery

Sometimes a query is any of the CRUD functions: INSERT, SELECT, UP-DATE, DELETE - and sometimes the word is taken more literally - meaning "question" - as opposed to "command" - and then only means the SELECT. When it comes to the naming of ADO.net functions, Microsoft has chosen the latter view. The *ExecuteNonQuery* is thus used for INSERT, UPDATE and DELETE where there is no data returned.

One of the simplest functions in TimeReg is "insertIntoMyProjects" which inserts a pair of foreign surrogate keys into the association/junction table MyProjects. This is found in Listing 7.1. We will examine this, as it has several generally usable patterns.

Lines 3 and 4 show the SQL text-string. This we already saw in Listing 4.3 in Chapter 4. Note that it is possible to add several VALUES pairs, using a comma in-between. This is however, typically not practical in normal code looping through objects.

Listing 7.1: Insert into MyProjects

```
1  public static void insertIntoMyProjects(int ProjectID, int EmployeeID)
2  {
3      string sql = "INSERT_INTO_MyProjects_(ProjectID,_EmployeeID)_"+
4                  "VALUES_(@ProjectID,_@EmployeeID)";
5
6      using (conn = new SqlConnection(LocalConnectionStr))
7      {
8          try
9          {
10             conn.Open();
11             if (conn.State == ConnectionState.Closed)
12                 return;
13         }
14         catch (SqlException)
15         {
16             System.Windows.Forms.MessageBox.Show
17             ("Exception_opening_SQL_Server_using:\n\r" +
18              LocalPublicConnectionStr);
19             return;
20         }
21
22         using (SqlCommand cmd = new SqlCommand(sql, conn))
23         {
24             cmd.Parameters.AddWithValue("@ProjectID", ProjectID);
25             cmd.Parameters.AddWithValue("@EmployeeID", EmployeeID);
26
27             try
28             {
29                 cmd.ExecuteNonQuery();
30             }
31             catch (SqlException e)
32             {
33                 System.Windows.Forms.MessageBox.Show
34                 (e.ToString() + "\n\rStacktrace:\n\r" + e.StackTrace,
35                 "Could_not_INSERT_data_into_MyProjects");
36             }
37         }
38     }
39 }
```

In line 6 an *SqlConnection* object is created. The tricky thing here is the actual connection-string, which we covered in Section 4.8

The *using* keyword is a clever standard C# construct, assuring that the object created goes out of scope at the closing "}" brace, and thus leaves us without worries about garbage collection. In the case of the SqlConnection object it is more complex, as ADO.net gives us *connection pooling* underneath it all.

In other words - it may look as if we for every (non-)query open a connection to the database, and then close it again. In reality ADO.net manages a pool of open connections for us. Nice.

In line 22 an *SqlCommand* object is created - here named "cmd". This uses the above sql string and the connection object. Again we see the use of "using". Thus, we don't need to worry about cleaning up after using the SqlCommand-object.

In lines 24 and 25, the two function input parameters - ProjectID and EmployeeID - are used to create two *SqlParameters*, which are inserted into an *SqlParameterCollection* in the recently created SqlCommand object. This is very compact code.

In line 29 the function ExecuteNonQuery is called on the SqlCommandObject.

All the SqlXXX objects/classes are part of ADO.net.

The only thing left to say is that we also use *try-catch* to feed errors back to the user.

As stated, the ExecuteNonQuery is almost identical to this INSERT when it comes to DELETE and UPDATE. The only real difference is in the initial SQL string.

7.3 ExecuteScalar

You might remember from Subsection 4.2.1 that we have an INSERT where we want the "identity" primary key which is incremented by SQL Server. We really need something like the above ExecuteNonQuery - but with a single output value. Knowing that a single value is also called a *scalar*, it is not a big surprise that we need *ExecuteScalar*. The pattern for handling this is almost the same as the ExecuteNonQuery. Listing 7.2 shows the few differences (apart from the fact that we now have five parameters instead of two).

Listing 7.2: Insert into Main

```
1  public static int insertNewMainRow(int employeeID, DateTime date,
2                     int projectID, float hours, string comment)
3  {
4      string sql =
5              "INSERT INTO Main "+
6              "   (EmployeeID, Date, ProjectID, Hours, Comment) "+
7              "OUTPUT INSERTED.MainID "+
8              "VALUES (@EmployeeID, @Date, @ProjectID, @Hours, @Comment)";
9
10 // Code removed
11         ID = (int)cmd.ExecuteScalar();
12 // Code removed
13         return ID;
14 }
```

7.4 ExecuteReader

Now for the SELECT. This may return lots of data, so we need some kind of inner loop where we can offload the individual rows of the result.

Listing 7.3 is a lot more complex than the DBUtil-code we have seen so-far. It is also more algorithmic complex than most functions in this layer. The reason is that the layers are not quite kept here. Some business domain logic that clearly belongs in the Model layer is "sneaked into" the database-interface.

Basically the reason is that this is where the code has first contact with every single row in an inner loop. It was tempting to do a little extra work here to get data better organized from start. It would be more clean to have these parts in the Model layer. But really not simpler. Making your own custom database-layer gives you this kind of freedom. This is also the main reason why it is shown here - it is a part of the story about adapting data from database to business model. It is used in function "selectWeekOf" in the Model layer - see Listing 6.6.

Getting back to the database agenda, we recognize at first glance, the overall structure: First the SQL, then "using" with SqlConnection as well as with SqlCommand.

Note the "ORDER BY ProjectID" in the SQL. This assures that we receive all data from a given project before data from other projects - essential for line 62.

The new part of the pattern - relating to SELECT - is the new inner-loop, where each round in the loop gives us a new row from the result of the SELECT. This is based on the *ExecuteReader* in line 50. For the "comment" parameter we need to make sure we don't try to read something with a NULL value.

The inner loop could be improved. We get the individual columns by their index in the original SQL SELECT. Instead of this manual indexing, it is possible to use the function *GetOrdinal(< ColumnName >)* on the *SqlDataReader* object. This uses extra CPU-cycles, but on the other hand is much more maintenance-friendly. We will meet this later.

The really new stuff is the use of the data-classes - or data transfer objects - that we will dig into later in this chapter. Normally a single data class is used, but in this complex function we use two - "CellData" and "Week". The general pattern in the functions based on SELECT and ExecuteReader is that data is inserted into the data-object by use of its *constructor*. This allows all properties to be set in one call. This is what we see here with CellData in lines 79-83. The containment hierarchy of all these objects is described in Chapter 6 and shown back in Figure 6.1.

The last thing to notice is the innocent call to *Sort* in line 107. This is only possible when the class is based on the C#-Interface IComparable as we shall see in Section 8.2.

Listing 7.3: Create List from database

```
1   public static List<Week> createListFromDB(
2                       DateTime firstday, int employeeID)
3   {
4       string sql = "SELECT␣M.MainID,␣M.Date,␣M.ProjectID,␣M.Hours,␣"+
5                    "␣␣␣M.Comment,␣M.InOracle,␣P.Parent,␣P.Name␣" +
6                    "FROM␣Main␣AS␣M,␣Projects␣AS␣P␣" +
7                    "WHERE␣M.EmployeeID␣=␣@EmployeeID␣␣" +
8                    "␣␣␣AND␣P.ProjectID␣=␣M.ProjectID␣" +
9                    "␣␣␣AND␣Date␣>=␣@Firstday␣AND␣Date␣<=␣@Lastday␣" +
10                   "ORDER␣BY␣M.ProjectID,␣M.Date";
11
12      List<Week> mainList = new List<Week>();
13
14      using (conn = new SqlConnection(LocalConnectionStr))
15      {
16          try
17          {
18              conn.Open();
19              if (conn.State == ConnectionState.Closed)
20                  return mainList;
21          }
22          catch (SqlException)
23          {
24              System.Windows.Forms.MessageBox.Show(
25              "Exception␣opening␣SQL␣Server␣using:\n\r" +
26               LocalPublicConnectionStr);
27              return mainList;
28          }
29
30          using (SqlCommand cmd = new SqlCommand(sql, conn))
31          {
32              cmd.Parameters.AddWithValue("@EmployeeID", employeeID);
33              cmd.Parameters.AddWithValue("@Firstday", firstday);
34              cmd.Parameters.AddWithValue("@Lastday", firstday.AddDays(6));
35
36              Week projectWeek = null;
37
38              int mainID = 0;
39              DateTime date;
40              int projectID = 0;
41              int oldProjectID = 0;
42              float hours = 0;
43              string comment = null;
44              int parentID = 0;
45              string name = null;
46              bool inOracle = false;
47
48              try
49              {
50                  SqlDataReader rdr = cmd.ExecuteReader();
51                  while (rdr.Read())
52                  {
53                      mainID = rdr.GetInt32(0);
54                      date = rdr.GetDateTime(1);
55                      projectID = rdr.GetInt32(2);
56                      hours = rdr.GetFloat(3);
```

```
57              comment = (rdr.IsDBNull(4)) ? "" : rdr.GetString(4);
58              inOracle = (!rdr.IsDBNull(5));
59              parentID = rdr.GetInt32(6);
60              name = rdr.GetString(7);
61
62              if (oldProjectID != projectID)
63              {
64                  // At this point we are for sure starting
65                  // a new week (not necessarily with data
66                  // from monday though
67                  oldProjectID = projectID;
68                  projectWeek = new Week(name);
69                  // 7 new days of references to CellData
70
71                  // Create a Project Row for a full week
72                  // with the given data
73                  DateTime day = firstday;
74
75                  // Create a weekfull of readonly
76                  // and "empty" data for now
77                  for (int weekday = 0; weekday < 7; weekday++)
78                  {
79                      projectWeek[weekday] = new CellData(
80                          day.AddDays(weekday),
81                          employeeID,
82                          projectID,
83                          parentID);
84                  }
85                  // Add the entry
86                  mainList.Add(projectWeek);
87              }
88
89              int dayInx = date.DayOfWeek - firstday.DayOfWeek;
90              if (dayInx == -1)    // Watch out for sundays!
91                  dayInx = 6;
92              projectWeek[dayInx].MainID = mainID;
93              projectWeek[dayInx].Hours = hours;
94              projectWeek[dayInx].Comment = comment;
95              projectWeek[dayInx].InOracle = inOracle;
96          }
97          rdr.Close();
98      }
99      catch (Exception e)
100     {
101         System.Windows.Forms.MessageBox.Show(e.ToString() +
102         "\n\rStacktrace:\n\r" + e.StackTrace,
103         "Could not read from Main");
104     }
105
106     // Sort according to projects and their parents
107     mainList.Sort();
108     return mainList;
109     }
110   }
111 }
```

7.5   SqlDataAdapter

As described earlier I have in another project used the *TableAdapter* framework. I rejected this because all the surrounding wizardry obscured what was happening. However, it is possible to work with adapters in a more classic coding style. ADO.net can be used with the same "intro" pattern that we saw in the previous section, but instead of an inner-loop with a reader, ADO.net can fill an un-typed *DataSet* or a subcomponent of this - a *DataTable*. To do this it uses *SqlDataAdapter*. With the *Fill* command, the SELECT is run and the DataTable is filled with the result.

This DataTable can be bound to a UI-element and changes can even be fed back to the database in the right mixture of DELETE, UPDATE and INSERT. This is extremely code-effective - especially if you are working on a single flat table. If the DataTable is filled from several tables using joins, update becomes more complex, and requires assistance from you.

For the TimeReg project I did not go down this path. Instead, I tried the SqlDataAdapter in a simple scenario. Listing 7.4 shows a simple query that finds the project name for a given ProjectID - the primary key in projects. In this case we expect exactly one row, but that doesn't change the principle.

In line 43 the name is returned. Note how, this time, the name of the column is used as index. This line also needs a "ToString()" as the DataTable knows nothing about types.

In the end the code in Listing 7.4 was not really used. Even with adapters this is a lot of work to get a project name - and then something similar must be coded if the parent-name is needed etc. It would mean a lot of trips to the database. Instead, I decided to maintain a "projects" dictionary in the DBUtil utility layer for all these simple lookups. It would have been more correct to keep it in the Model layer. Linq is formidable for searches in this.

The SqlDataAdapter and its friends, the DataSet and the DataTable, are more performance hungry than the SqlDataReader. This should not be a surprise. The reader only allows for reading from one end to another, while the adapter-components supports updates back to the database and other advanced features.

Listing 7.4: Using SqlDataAdapter in a limited way

```
1   public static string projectName(int projectID)
2   {
3       string sql = "SELECT_Name_FROM_Projects_"+
4                     "WHERE_ProjectID_=_@ProjectID";
5
6       using (conn = new SqlConnection(LocalConnectionStr))
7       {
8           try
9           {
10              conn.Open();
11              if (conn.State == ConnectionState.Closed)
12                  return "";
13          }
14          catch (SqlException)
15          {
16              System.Windows.Forms.MessageBox.Show
17              ("Exception_opening_SQL_Server_using:\n\r"
18               + LocalPublicConnectionStr);
19              return "";
20          }
21
22          using (SqlCommand cmd = new SqlCommand(sql, conn))
23          {
24              cmd.Parameters.AddWithValue("@ProjectID", projectID);
25              SqlDataAdapter adapter = new SqlDataAdapter();
26              adapter.SelectCommand = cmd;
27
28              DataTable projtable = new DataTable();
29              try
30              {
31                  adapter.Fill(projtable);
32              }
33              catch (Exception e)
34              {
35                  System.Windows.Forms.MessageBox.Show
36                  (e.ToString() + "\n\rStacktrace:\n\r" +
37                  e.StackTrace, "Could_not_fill_Table_from_Projects");
38                  return "";
39              }
40
41              if (projtable.Rows.Count == 1)
42              {
43                  return projtable.Rows[0]["Name"].ToString();
44              }
45              else if (projtable.Rows.Count > 1)
46              {
47                  System.Windows.Forms.MessageBox.Show
48                  ("Database_Integrity_Problem_"
49                   + "-_more_projects_with_same_ProjectID");
50                  return "";
51              }
52              else
53                  return "";
54  }}} // saving space...
```

7.6   Oracle Managed Data Access

I have stated many times that *Oracle Managed Data Access* is modeled after ADO.net. This means that coding against Oracle is not much different from coding against SQL Server - at least when the previously shown patterns are used.

Listing 7.5 is a proof of this statement. It is a simple query, selecting the interesting columns of all projects in the relevant Oracle table. The fact that this table - apps.comp_projects - actually is a View, changes nothing. The SQL statement in lines 3 and 4 is exactly the same as it would be in SQL Server. This is because it is a SELECT - an INSERT e.g., looks a bit different from the ones we have seen.

In line 7 we see the usual "using" - creating a *Connection* object, with the help of a defined connection-string. In lines 26-28 we open a *Command* object on the *Connection* object. Again this is "packed within a using statement". In line 33 we *ExecuteReader* on the command object. In line 34 we loop on this reader, accessing strings and DateTime objects by indexes that originates from the position in the SQL text. In-between, exceptions are handled - should they arise.

The above description completely matches that of a similar use of ExecuteReader in ADO.net. Looking at the code the only difference is that instead of the ADO objects we now use objects from Oracle's Managed-DataAccess namespace.

Listing 7.5: Oracle Managed Data Access

```
 1  public static List<ProjInfo> getOracleProjects()
 2  {
 3      string SQL = "SELECT_PROJECT_NAME,_PROJECT_NUMBER,_"+
 4                  "START_DATE,_END_DATE_FROM_apps.comp_projects";
 5      List<ProjInfo> result = new List<ProjInfo>();
 6
 7      using (conn = new Oracle.ManagedDataAccess.Client.
 8          OracleConnection(connString))
 9      {
10          try
11          {
12              conn.Open();
13              if (conn.State == System.Data.ConnectionState.Closed)
14                  return result;
15          }
16          catch (Oracle.ManagedDataAccess.Client.OracleException exc)
17          {
18              System.Windows.Forms.MessageBox.Show(
19                  "Exception_opening_Oracle-server:_" +
20                  exc.Message + "\r\nInner_Exc:" +
21                  exc.InnerException + "Stack:\r\n" +
22                  exc.StackTrace);
23              return result;
24          }
25
26          using (Oracle.ManagedDataAccess.Client.OracleCommand
27              cmd = new
28              Oracle.ManagedDataAccess.Client.OracleCommand(SQL,conn))
29          {
30              try
31              {
32                  Oracle.ManagedDataAccess.Client.
33                      OracleDataReader rdr = cmd.ExecuteReader();
34                  while (rdr.Read())
35                      result.Add(new ProjInfo(
36                          rdr.GetOracleString(0).ToString(), // name
37                          rdr.GetOracleString(1).ToString(), // number
38                          (rdr.IsDBNull(2)) ? new DateTime(1990,1,1) :
39                          rdr.GetOracleDate(2).Value,  // Start_date
40                          (rdr.IsDBNull(3)) ? new DateTime(2200,1,1) :
41                          rdr.GetOracleDate(3).Value)); // End_date
42              }
43              catch (Oracle.ManagedDataAccess.Client.OracleException exc)
44              {
45                  System.Windows.Forms.MessageBox.Show(exc.ToString() +
46                      "\n\rStacktrace:\n\r" + exc.StackTrace);
47                  return result;
48              }
49
50              return result;
51          }
52      }
53  }
```

Chapter 8

Data Transfer Objects

8.1 CellData Class

It is time to look at the data-classes or data transfer objects. We start with "CellData" which represents all data to and from the database that end up in a single cell in the main view in TimeReg. This is later used by "Week" which is a class that represents a week of data from a given project.

CellData is shown in Listing 8.1. The first thing we note is the member variables in lines 3-9, and how they have different access modifiers. Some are even *readonly*. This does not sound very productive. The point is that they are readonly - once created. This means that they are initialized in the constructor and from hereon cannot be changed. The ones that are *protected* may be changed by the class itself. This is done in *properties*. Note that it is possible to create properties directly without underlying member variables. This is the case for "Changed" and "InOracle".

You might argue that instead of all the above we could simply just have public member-variables. After all - this class is for moving data in and out of a database. No encapsulation here. However, we want to use CellData with databinding to UI-classes - and they look for properties - not member-variables. When you allow a UI-object to mess with your data, it makes sense to only allow it to write where it needs to.

The constructor is created so that it is easy to use on dummy-data - cells that are ready for data from the user. Thus, it always sets the "MainID" - the primary key for the row - to -1. If the constructor is used on data fetched from the database, the MainID must be set explicitly afterwards. The same applies for Changed and InOracle.

Listing 8.1: CellData - one project on one day

```
 1  public class CellData
 2  {
 3      protected int       m_mainID;
 4      readonly  int       m_employeeID;
 5      readonly  int       m_parentID;
 6      readonly  DateTime  m_date;
 7      readonly  int       m_projectID;
 8      protected float     m_hours;
 9      protected string    m_comment;
10
11      public CellData(DateTime date, int employeeID,
12                      int projectID, int parentID)
13      {
14          m_date       = date;
15          m_employeeID = employeeID;
16          m_projectID  = projectID;
17          m_parentID   = parentID;
18          m_mainID     = -1;
19          m_hours      = 0;
20          m_comment    = "";
21
22          Changed      = false;
23          InOracle     = false;
24      }
25
26      public int MainID      { get { return m_mainID; }
27                               set { m_mainID = value; } }
28      public int EmployeeID  { get { return m_employeeID; } }
29      public DateTime Date   { get { return m_date; } }
30      public int ProjectID   { get { return m_projectID; } }
31      public int ParentID    { get { return m_parentID; } }
32      public float Hours     { get { return m_hours; }
33                               set { m_hours = value; } }
34      public string Comment  { get { return m_comment; }
35                               set { m_comment = value; } }
36      public bool Changed    { get; set; }
37      public bool InOracle   { get; set; }
38  }
```

8.2   Week Class

The "Week" class is a very simple data class. It is shown in Listing 8.2. Week contains a "CellData" object for each day of the week, and a string with the project-name - common to all the cells. It is however imperative that it can be used in sorted lists - as seen in Section 7.4. C# sorts for you - if you define the single function of IComparable: *CompareTo*. This function always takes as input an object of the same class as being called - here called "other". In this case it calls a static function that hierarchically compares two projects - first by their parents, then by themselves. This is generally used.

If you want to use an object in a dictionary, CompareTo is not enough. You also need a function called *GetHashCode*. This should return something as unique as possible. Since ProjectID is a primary key, it is as unique as it can be. So GetHashCode is *overridden*. This means that this method will be used instead of the default implementation which cannot always be trusted.

The final handy function in the comparing-domain is *Equals*. This is also overridden.

Together these three functions allow the application programmer to write some neat code. It is good practice to implement them - at least when you plan to use *collections*. You cannot always foresee when C# decides to call the methods that are overridden here.

Actually, all three implementations have a small flaw. Two Week objects could contain the same project - but for different dates. The way TimeReg works, these Week objects are only in a common list when they belong to the same calendar week. Still, it is an error waiting to happen.

Another interesting thing in Listing 8.2 is the declaration in lines 41-52. With this code, a Week-based object can reference the embedded CellData objects directly as array-elements of the Week-based object:

```
float hours = projectWeek[0].Hours;
```

The above code gives us the hours spent Monday on the specific project.

Listing 8.2: Week with IComparable interface

```
1   public class Week : IComparable<Week>
2   {
3       private CellData[] Days = new CellData[7];
4       private string projectName;
5
6       public string ProjectName { get { return projectName; }
7                                   set { projectName = value; } }
8
9       public Week(string projectName)
10      {
11          this.projectName = projectName;
12      }
13
14      private Week()
15      {
16      }
17
18      public int CompareTo(Week other)
19      {
20          if (other == null) return 1;
21
22          return DBUtil.CompareTwo(this[0].ProjectID,
23                  this[0].ParentID, other[0].ProjectID, other[0].ParentID);
24      }
25
26      public override bool Equals(object obj)
27      {
28          if (obj == null || obj.GetType() != GetType())
29              return false;
30
31          Week otherweek = obj as Week;
32
33          return (otherweek[0].ProjectID == this[0].ProjectID &&
34                  otherweek[0].Date == this[0].Date);
35      }
36
37      public override int GetHashCode()
38      {
39          return this[0].ProjectID;
40      }
41      public CellData this[int index]
42      {
43          get
44          {
45              return Days[index];
46          }
47
48          set
49          {
50              Days[index] = value;
51          }
52      }
53  }
```

8.3 Classic Class Concept

The DBUtil layer presented so far is made up of static functions for doing the actual SQL-commands, and nested classes, instantiated into objects, holding and transporting the data. The nice thing about this concept is that a given nested data-class can be reused by several static functions. This is indeed used.

As described in Section 4.5, forecasts were introduced in the TimeReg application after a year or so. Just for the fun of it, I decided that this time I would use a more classic object-oriented approach: Now SQL-commands would take place from within instantiated classes (not static), and these classes would also do all the data-mapping.

Listing all the code would take up too much space, but you are welcome to download the code and have a look.

Naturally this also works. There is a tendency towards these classes becoming more "model-heavy". Probably because they each are their own data transfer object - so to speak. The fact that this data part is inside the class instead of outside - possibly shared with other classes - allows for more specific handling. This is the whole idea of object orientation, and is absolutely not a problem.

8.4 A Dapper alternative

As stated earlier, it is easy to get caught up in Microsoft's "legacy land". Maintenance is one reason to avoid today's flavor of framework. Another reason is that frameworks tend to be too helpful, which makes them huge and complex, and thus difficult to customize.

This has left an open field for minor *ORM - object relational mapping -* tools. One such tool that shows promise is *Dapper*. "Dapper" is an adjective that e.g. in old Hollywood movies was used about a man. Synonyms are "dashing", "neat" and "well groomed". Dapper is invented by the developers at *StackOverflow -* a fantastic site for all us developers. If you know StackOverflow, you also know that it works fast and efficient. The

Listing 8.3: Dapper Query

```
1  // The connection has been opened like we have seen before
2  var queryRes = conn.query<Project>("SELECT ProjectID, Name, ProjectNo
3  FROM dbo.Projects WHERE ProjectID = @ProjectID",
4  new{ @ProjectID = 1012 });
```

basic concept in Dapper is that you write data-classes - pretty much like the ones in this chapter. Dapper takes the role of an ADO SqlConnection class by extending its *IDbConnection* interface with e.g. a *Query* method. This new method takes your data-class as a template. Thus, instead of writing specific functions like I have shown earlier, it is possible to write much more condensed code like Listing 8.3 - where "conn" is an SqlConnection:

It is even possible to escape the templated class and instead use "dynamic" objects. This can be handy for simple "hipshot" test-scripts, but most will probably prefer the typed approach.

Dapper basically only supports SELECT, but there are 3'rd party extensions supporting DELETE, UPDATE and INSERT. Obviously this brings us close to the aforementioned maintenance-nightmare, but there is a certain beauty in the "Dapper" approach.

Chapter 9

UI Design

9.1 ListBox

Databinding is the concept of linking a *DataSource* such as a database to a UI-element - e.g. a *List* or a *DataGrid*. It can be one way - reading data into the UI-element - or it may be both ways, which also means writing stuff back to the base. You can always find sample-applications that work both ways, however in real-life it is rarely the case - nor optimal. Typically, a lot of data is read, while only a few items are written back - and often these few items need some kind of translation or validation first.

Listing 9.1: Very simple databinding

```
 1  namespace TimeReg
 2  {
 3      internal partial class MyProjects : Form
 4      {
 5          private Model model;
 6          private List<DBUtil.ProjTupple> myProjects = null;
 7
 8          public void updateMyProjects()
 9          {
10              myProjects = DBUtil.myProjects(model.MyID);
11              lstMyProjs.DataSource = myProjects;
12              lstMyProjs.DisplayMember = "Name";
13              lstMyProjs.Refresh();
14          }
```

Sometimes databinding can be as simple as shown in Listing 9.1. In line 10 the static function DBUtil.myProjects queries the database and fills a local list with all the projects the user has registered as his. Each item in this list is a "ProjectTupple" with all relevant information about the project. In line 11 the list is handed to a UI *ListBox* - "lstMyProjs" - as DataSource. This effectively fills the ListBox with the ProjectTupples. In line 12 the ListBox *DisplayMember* is set to "Name". This is how we tell the ListBox that it shall display the field from ProjectTupple called "Name" in the UI.

This simple databinding is very powerful. Not only do we fill the list with what we want to show the user, we also have all other relevant information with us in the list. When the user later has selected a number of items in the list, it is equally simple to delete these if the user chooses so. Still, as stated earlier, the delete action does not happen directly via the databinding in TimeReg. As Listing 9.2 shows, the event-handler loops through all selected items, asking DBUtil.deleteFromMyProjects to delete the relevant projectIDs from the table, based on the extra information carried in the ProjTupple within each item.

Listing 9.2: Using hidden data

```
1  private void btnFromMyProjs_Click(object sender, EventArgs e)
2  {
3      foreach (DBUtil.ProjTupple item in lstMyProjs.SelectedItems)
4          DBUtil.deleteFromMyProjects(item.ProjectID, model.MyID);
5
6      updateMyProjects();
7  }
```

Listing 9.3 from the ReportsDlg.cs goes a little further.

Listing 9.3: Extending the List

```
1      // Make a list with all projects and a fake ALL in front
2      allProjs = DBUtil.getAllProjects();
3      allProjs.Insert(0, new DBUtil.ProjTupple(
4          0, "All", 0, "", false,"", 0,"ALL","","All"));
5      lstMyOnly.DataSource = allProjs;
6      lstMyOnly.ValueMember = "Name";
7      lstMyOnly.DisplayMember = "Name";
8      lstMyOnly.DropDownStyle = ComboBoxStyle.DropDownList;
9      lstMyOnly.MouseWheel += new MouseEventHandler(List_MouseWheel);
10     lstMyOnly.Enabled = false;
11
12 //Code skipped...
13 void List_MouseWheel(object sender, MouseEventArgs e)
14 {
15     ((HandledMouseEventArgs)e).Handled = true;
16 }
```

Here we change the style to *DropDownList* and attach the mouse-wheel event. In this case to assure that we do *not* get the default mouse-scroll in the list which can be very annoying. However, we also use the indirect databinding to insert a "fake" project at the top of the local list before it is attached as DataSource.

9.2 DataGridView

The dominating class used with databases is *DataGridView*. This is a very clever - but also huge class. It has tons of data-members, functions and events. In this section we will continue the ongoing sample from the previous chapters. As you may remember, we built a "locallist" which is a local shadow containing the data we need to show in the main view. The class for this dialog is UserView.cs, and the DataGridView instance is simply called "grid". Thus event-handlers are by default named "grid_< *event* >" by Visual Studio.

In the following subsections we will examine the most important functions related to this grid.

9.2.1 Initialize Grid

The grid is declared in the Visual Studio *Designer*. Listing 9.4 shows the auto-generated lines from the designer that are not related to positions, anchoring etc. The main agenda is to make windows draw the grid decently and not to allow users to delete or rearrange columns and rows.

After the designer-generated code, the final initialization is "setupGrid" found in Listing 9.5. Here the headers are named, and disabling of user-intervention continues by making all columns non-sortable. Columns for Saturday and Sunday are grayed. Later we shall see that various holidays are also grayed. Input of hours is, by the way, not disabled in weekends and on holidays - except for sickness and vacation which does not make sense here.

Listing 9.4: Designer Initialization

```
1   this.grid.AllowUserToAddRows = false;
2   this.grid.AllowUserToDeleteRows = false;
3   this.grid.AllowUserToResizeRows = false;
4   this.grid.AutoSizeColumnsMode = System.Windows.Forms.
5       DataGridViewAutoSizeColumnsMode.Fill;
6   this.grid.AutoSizeRowsMode = System.Windows.Forms.
7       DataGridViewAutoSizeRowsMode.AllCells;
8   this.grid.ColumnHeadersHeightSizeMode = System.Windows.Forms.
9       DataGridViewColumnHeadersHeightSizeMode.AutoSize;
10  this.grid.MultiSelect = false;
11  this.grid.RowHeadersWidthSizeMode = System.Windows.Forms.
12      DataGridViewRowHeadersWidthSizeMode.AutoSizeToDisplayedHeaders;
13  this.grid.RowTemplate.Height = 24;
14  this.grid.Size = new System.Drawing.Size(1020, 400);
15  this.grid.TabIndex = 0;
16  this.grid.CellMouseClick += new System.Windows.Forms.
17      DataGridViewCellMouseEventHandler(this.grid_CellMouseClick);
18  this.grid.CellValueChanged += new System.Windows.Forms.
19      DataGridViewCellEventHandler(this.grid_CellValueChanged);
20  this.grid.EditingControlShowing += new System.Windows.Forms.
21      DataGridViewEditingControlShowingEventHandler(
22          this.grid_EditingControlShowing);
```

Listing 9.5: Coded Setup

```
1   private void setupGrid()
2   {
3       grid.ColumnCount = 8;
4       grid.Columns[0].Name = "Project";
5       grid.Columns[1].Name = "Monday";
6       grid.Columns[2].Name = "Tuesday";
7       grid.Columns[3].Name = "Wednesday";
8       grid.Columns[4].Name = "Thursday";
9       grid.Columns[5].Name = "Friday";
10      grid.Columns[6].Name = "Saturday";
11      grid.Columns[7].Name = "Sunday";
12
13      // Change the headers of weekends and Projects
14      grid.EnableHeadersVisualStyles = false;
15      grid.Columns["Project"].HeaderCell.Style.BackColor =
16          Color.LightGray;
17      grid.Columns["Saturday"].HeaderCell.Style.BackColor =
18          Color.LightGray;
19      grid.Columns["Sunday"].HeaderCell.Style.BackColor =
20          Color.LightGray;
21
22      foreach (DataGridViewColumn col in grid.Columns)
23          col.SortMode = DataGridViewColumnSortMode.NotSortable;
24
25      grid.ShowCellToolTips = true;
26  }
```

9.2.2 Update Grid

A very central function is "updateGridFromTable" - see Listing 9.6. This function is called whenever we need new data from the database. Thus, it is called when the page is first shown (after initialization), but also when the user moves to another week, or decides to cancel existing entries. It is also called if the user has updated his list of projects or has switched database. If the user is a superuser, he or she might "alias" as another user to fill in missing data, in which case we also need updateGridFromTable. This function takes as input the relevant Monday of the week to fetch, and in line 12 calls the relevant function in the Model - "selectWeekOf". This fills the "locallist" from the database as we saw in Chapter 6.

The basic functionality of updateGridFromTable is not hard to follow, and the comments help. There are however, some tricks that might need some explanations:

In line 8 the class flag "suspendCellValueChanged" is set to true. The grid is wired up to call an event-handler "grid_CellValueChanged" whenever the user has updated a cell. It is however also called when a cell value is programmatically changed. As we will see in Subsection 9.2.3, this event-handler may cause changes to the contents of the same or other cells (sums) - which fires the same event-handler again. The code is not re-entrant, so this could easily give some nasty effects - apart from wasting a lot of CPU cycles. The event might also get triggered while our updateGridFromTable is run, which also can give problems. Thus, the flag "suspendCellVal-ueChanged" is introduced. It is set to true when entering either of these functions, and set back to false when leaving. If the flag is already set when entering the event-handler nothing is done. An alternative solution is to remove the event-handler instead of setting the flag, and re-install it instead of clearing the flag. It is also possible that Microsoft has a "disable" flag somewhere that I haven't found; once a problem is solved you don't search so hard for alternative solutions.

In lines 58 to 64 the grid's autosize parameters are stored before they are disabled, and in lines 130 and 131 they are set back to their original values. This speeds up the update of the grid.

Note the "magic numbers" for the index of various weekdays and loop-counters based on these. Hard-coded numbers are normally considered bad design, but when it comes to such elementary things as the number of days in a week etc., we can count on these not to change. In such cases I find that numbers are easier to read than named constants.

The holiday-dictionary from the Model layer is used. If a given date has a matching holiday, the header gets a gray background and the name of the holiday is used instead of the weekday.

Listing 9.6: updateGridFromTable

```
1   private void updateGridFromTable(DateTime monday)
2   {
3       // User must be verified
4       if (model.MyID == 0)
5           return;
6
7       // Avoid re-entrancy issues - set flag to "suspend" event
8       suspendCellValueChanged = true;
9
10      // Fill the local "shadow" via the model
11      int weekno;
12      localList = model.selectWeekOf(monday, out weekno);
13      lblWeekNo.Text = "Week:_" + weekno.ToString() + "_(EU/ISO)";
14
15      // Start a new week
16      grid.Rows.Clear();
17
18      int gridRowCount;
19
20      // Setup the headers - even if there are no data,
21      // we need to see the dates to navigate
22      // Use weekday-name in general - but holiday if it exists
23      grid.Columns[0].HeaderText = "Project";
24
25      DateTime day = monday;
26      for (int i = 0; i < 7; i++)
27      {
28          string name;
29          if (model.holidayDict.TryGetValue(day, out name))
30          {
31              // Use name of holiday and Paint gray
32              grid.Columns[i + 1].HeaderCell.Style.BackColor = holiday;
33          }
34          else
35          {
36              // Use weekday name and Paint normal - remembering weekends
37              if (i < 5)
38                  grid.Columns[i + 1].HeaderCell.Style.BackColor = workday;
39              name = day.DayOfWeek.ToString();
40          }
41
42          grid.Columns[i + 1].HeaderText =
43              name + "\n" + day.ToShortDateString();
44          day = day.AddDays(1);
45      }
```

```
46
47      if (localList.Count() == 0)
48      {
49          grid.Columns[0].HeaderText = "No_Data";
50          suspendCellValueChanged = false;
51          return;
52      }
53
54      Font bold = new Font(grid.DefaultCellStyle.Font.Name,
55                          grid.DefaultCellStyle.Font.Size, FontStyle.Bold);
56
57      // Don't AutoSize when updating the grid
58      DataGridViewAutoSizeColumnsMode AutoSizeColMode =
59          grid.AutoSizeColumnsMode;
60      DataGridViewAutoSizeRowsMode AutoSizeRowsMode =
61          grid.AutoSizeRowsMode;
62
63      grid.AutoSizeRowsMode = DataGridViewAutoSizeRowsMode.None;
64      grid.AutoSizeColumnsMode = DataGridViewAutoSizeColumnsMode.None;
65
66      // Loop through the rows - each is a project
67      foreach (DBUtil.Week projectWeek in localList)
68      {
69          if (projectWeek == null)
70              break;
71
72          string[] row = new string[8];
73          // Very first column is ProjectID -
74          // -  should be the same for all cells - pick any one
75          int parentID = projectWeek[0].ParentID;
76
77          // First Column is Project Name
78          row[0] = projectWeek.ProjectName;
79
80          // Go through the weekdays - setting Hours
81          // Starting in Column 1 - leaving the Project Names in Column 0
82          for (int dayInx = 1; dayInx < 8; dayInx++)
83          {
84              float hours = projectWeek[dayInx-1].Hours;
85              row[dayInx] = (hours == 0.0) ? "" : hours.ToString();
86          }
87
88          // Now put it in the grid
89          grid.Rows.Add(row);
90          gridRowCount = grid.Rows.Count;
91
92          // Mark the parents bold
93          if (parentID <= 0)
94              grid.Rows[grid.RowCount-1].Cells[0].Style.Font = bold;
95
96          // Go through the weekdays - setting Tooltips to Comments
97          // And make read-only if value is transferred to Oracle
98          // .. or if the day is a non-working day
99          //    and the project is absence
100         for (int dayInx = 1; dayInx < 8; dayInx++)
101         {
102             grid.Rows[gridRowCount-1].Cells[dayInx].ToolTipText =
```

```
103                    projectWeek[dayInx-1].Comment;
104            if (projectWeek[dayInx-1].InOracle ||
105               (projectWeek[dayInx-1].ParentID < 0 &&
106               grid.Columns[dayInx].HeaderCell.Style.BackColor
107                  == holiday))
108            {
109                grid.Rows[gridRowCount-1].Cells[dayInx].ReadOnly =
110                  true;
111                grid.Rows[gridRowCount-1].Cells[dayInx].Style.BackColor =
112                  readOnly;
113            }
114         }
115      }
116
117      // Calculate AND create a sum row
118      grid.Rows.Add(calcSumRow(false));
119      grid.Rows[grid.RowCount-1].ReadOnly = true;
120      grid.Rows[grid.RowCount-1].DefaultCellStyle.BackColor =
121         Color.LightGray;
122      grid.Rows[grid.RowCount-1].DefaultCellStyle.SelectionBackColor =
123         Color.LightGray;
124      grid.Rows[grid.RowCount-1].DefaultCellStyle.SelectionForeColor =
125         Color.Black;
126
127      // Size first column according to the text in it
128      grid.Columns["Project"].AutoSizeMode =
129         DataGridViewAutoSizeColumnMode.DisplayedCells;
130      // Finally - enable autosize again
131      grid.AutoSizeRowsMode = AutoSizeRowsMode;
132      grid.AutoSizeColumnsMode = AutoSizeColMode;
133      // Select the first project, first day
134      grid.Rows[0].Cells["Monday"].Selected = true;
135      grid.Columns["Project"].ReadOnly = true;
136
137      // allow for the event again
138      suspendCellValueChanged = false;
139   }
```

9.2.3 Edit in Grid

There are several event-handlers for the grid. One handler looks for a right-mouse click and allows the user to key in comments when this happens. Another is used to filter out unwanted characters in the input from the user, when actually editing. These and other handlers are not shown here to save space - but can be downloaded with the rest.

However, the main event-handler is shown in Listing 9.7. The function is named "grid_CellValueChanged" and is called whenever the user leaves a cell within the grid after having edited it. The use of "suspendCellValueChanged" is explained in the previous subsection.

In line 9 and 10, the current cell's row and column indexes are read. This is much easier than performing a hit-test. In line 14, empty strings are converted into the value 0. The Model layer will interpret a value changed to 0 as an SQL DELETE in the function updateDatabase.

Since this grid is the only part of the application that is used by many people on a daily basis, it must be easy to use. Hours are simply entered as normal decimal numbers. However, in Denmark the official decimal separator is ",", but programmers often use "." - and we also have people stationed in other countries. To avoid people getting error-messages all the time, the code must be forgiving and allow the user to use whatever he or she likes.

After some time a user asked me if he could enter time as hours:minutes. So this was also introduced - again by adapting to the input, as seen in line 21.

In line 71 we bail out if nothing is really changed. Beginning in line 81 the hours are accumulated and written. All sums are re-calculated. For performance reasons we might consider only updating the current column and the total, but it really isn't worth the risk of doing the sums in two different ways.

In line 87 the dirty flag is set. After this the Cancel and Submit buttons are updated. Since the dirty flag is set, they will now be active and colored (they might have been already before). Finally, we clear the suspendCellValueChanged flag.

Listing 9.7: CellValueChanged

```
1   private void grid_CellValueChanged(object sender,
2       DataGridViewCellEventArgs e)
3   {
4       if (!suspendCellValueChanged && grid.CurrentCell != null)
5       {
6           suspendCellValueChanged = true;
7
8           float val;
9           int row = grid.CurrentCell.RowIndex;
10          int col = grid.CurrentCell.ColumnIndex;
11
12          // If user deletes entries and then
13          //  moves with arrows we have a null value
14          if (grid.CurrentCell.Value == null ||
15              ((string)grid.CurrentCell.Value).Length == 0)
16          {
17              grid.CurrentCell.Value = "";
18              val = 0;
19          }
20
21          else if (grid.CurrentCell.Value.ToString().Contains(':'))
22          {
23              // Treat as Hours:Minutes
24              string fullTxt = grid.CurrentCell.Value.ToString();
25              string[] tokens = fullTxt.Split(':');
26              if (tokens.Length != 2)
27              {
28                  MessageBox.Show("When using ':' operator please supply"+
29                      " <Hours>:<Minutes> and nothing else",
30                       "Illegal Number-format");
31                  grid.CurrentCell.Value =
32                      localList[row][col - 1].Hours.ToString();
33                  suspendCellValueChanged = false;
34                  return;
35              }
36              int hours, minutes;
37              if (!int.TryParse(tokens[0], out hours) ||
38                  !int.TryParse(tokens[1], out minutes) || minutes >= 60)
39              {
40                  MessageBox.Show("When using ':' operator, hours and"+
41                      " minutes must be integers\r\n" +
42                      " - and minutes must be less than 60",
43                       "Illegal Number-format");
44                  grid.CurrentCell.Value =
45                      localList[row][col - 1].Hours.ToString();
46                  suspendCellValueChanged = false;
47                  return;
48              }
49              val = (float)hours + (float)minutes / (float)60;
50          }
51
52          else
53          {
54              // Allow people to use , or . as they please
55              string invStr = grid.CurrentCell.Value.
56                  ToString().Replace(',', '.');
```

```
57              if (!float.TryParse(invStr,NumberStyles.Any,
58                  CultureInfo.InvariantCulture, out val))
59              {
60                  MessageBox.Show("Cannot_parse:_"+
61                      grid.CurrentCell.Value.ToString(),
62                      "Illegal_Number-format");
63                  grid.CurrentCell.Value =
64                      localList[row][col - 1].Hours.ToString();
65                  suspendCellValueChanged = false;
66                  return;
67              }
68          }
69          // If the user has fiddled around
70          //- and made no change in the end - bail out
71          if (Math.Abs(localList[row][col - 1].Hours - val) < 0.01)
72          {
73              suspendCellValueChanged = false;
74              return;
75          }
76
77          localList[row][col - 1].Hours = val;
78          localList[row][col - 1].Changed = true;
79          grid.CurrentCell.Style.BackColor = dirty;
80
81          string [] ssum = calcSumRow(true);
82
83          for (int colInx = 0; colInx < grid.ColumnCount; colInx++)
84              grid.Rows[grid.RowCount - 1].Cells[colInx].Value =
85                  ssum[colInx];
86
87          model.Dirty = true;
88          updateButtons();
89          suspendCellValueChanged = false;
90      }
91  }
```

9.2.4 Submit to database

After all the hard work with the grid, the event-handler for the Submit button becomes very simple - see Listing 9.8.

The Model does the real work of traversing the grid and making the relevant DELETE, UPDATE or INSERT statements. It also clears the dirty flag, so that "updateButtons" works as it should, which is to make the buttons inactive.

Listing 9.8: Submit

```
1   private void btnSubmit_Click(object sender, EventArgs e)
2   {
3       // The localTable is already updated - send it to the database
4       model.updateDatabase();
5       // Give cells "unchanged background"
6       //- except the readonly which are the sums and those in oracle
7       foreach (DataGridViewRow row in grid.Rows)
8           if (!row.ReadOnly)
9               foreach (DataGridViewCell cell in row.Cells)
10                  if (!cell.ReadOnly)
11                      cell.Style.BackColor = Color.White;
12
13      updateButtons();
14  }
```

9.2.5 Double Buffering

The main view that we have spent so much time on, does not contain a lot of data and is very fast. This is not the case for the Reports view where employees and managers can get reports on e.g. hours spent on projects - per developer. A DataGridView is also used here, but it can have thousands of rows. It may save time when filling these rows to turn on *double buffering*.

The code for this is somewhat on the low-level side and is shown in Listing 9.9

Listing 9.9: Double Buffering

```
1   if (!System.Windows.Forms.SystemInformation.TerminalServerSession)
2   {
3       Type dgvType = grid.GetType();
4       PropertyInfo pi = dgvType.GetProperty("DoubleBuffered",
5           BindingFlags.Instance | BindingFlags.NonPublic);
6       pi.SetValue(grid, true, null);
7   }
```

9.2.6 Multiple uses of a single DataGridView

Let's take a closer look at the Report dialog. This is seen in Figure 9.1.

Figure 9.1: Reports Dialog

The Report dialog separates itself from other dialogs, by using a single DataGridView in several ways. This is not really difficult in itself, but it is easy to get lost in the many "if-then-else" that updates this grid according to various radio-buttons, drop-down-boxes etc. This problem is solved by the use of the following easy pattern:

Listing 9.10: Radio Button Handler

```
private void rdBtnTotalPerProjPerEmp_CheckedChanged(
    object sender, EventArgs e)
{
    if (((RadioButton)sender).Checked)
    {
        lblCategories.Enabled = cmbCategories.Enabled = true;
        reCalculate();
    }
}
```

❏ Each radio-button has a handler, that only does something when the button is checked. Thus, we do not care about all the buttons that become unchecked. The handler is responsible for turning on other UI-elements that are relevant for the specific scenario - and also for turning off those that are not. Listing 9.10 is called when the user asks to see a report on total hours per project per employee. In this case we want to enable a dropdown list with "categories". This can be used to filter on specific types of hours. Any handler ends by calling "reCalculate".

❏ The single reCalculate function collects all handler actions and spreads them again. reCalculate is seen in Listing 9.11. This again checks which radio-button is active, and calls the corresponding "datagrid filler". The extra check seems superfluous, but it simplifies the code a lot, by allowing reCalculate to be called from anywhere at anytime without any consideration to the current state.

❏ The relevant datagrid-filler function is called from reCalculate. Listing 9.12 shows updateTotalPerEmpsReport - corresponding to the radiobutton handler.

❏ Various filter functions for date-range, categories etc. may be called. They simply re-invoke the reCalculate function after setting the filter.

Listing 9.11: Recalculate from everywhere

```
 1  private void reCalculate()
 2  {
 3      if (rdBtnTotPerProj.Checked)
 4          updateTotalsReport();
 5      else if (rdBtnTotalPerProjPerEmp.Checked)
 6          updateTotalPerEmpsReport();
 7      else if (rdBtnTasksForMe.Checked)
 8          updatePersonalReport();
 9      else if (rdBtnTotPerParentProjs.Checked)
10          updateTotalsOnParentReport();
11      else if (rdBtnDaysAccounted.Checked)
12          updateDaysAccountedFor();
13
14      chkMonths.Enabled = (rdBtnTotPerParentProjs.Checked ||
15          rdBtnTotPerProj.Checked || rdBtnTotalPerProjPerEmp.Checked);
16  }
```

Listing 9.12: Datagrid Filler

```
1   private void updateTotalPerEmpsReport()
2   {
3       Cursor saveCursor = this.Cursor;
4       this.Cursor = Cursors.WaitCursor;
5
6       projectReport = DBUtil.getProjectTotalsPerEmployee(
7          dtFrom.Value.Date, dtTo.Value.Date, model.SuperUser);
8
9       // Filter out everything but the relevant category
10      if (!cmbCategories.Text.ToLower().Equals("all"))
11      {
12          List<DBUtil.ProjectReport> reportTemp =
13             new List<DBUtil.ProjectReport>();
14          // Get cat. by reverse lookup - then filter locally
15          string key = model.Categories.FirstOrDefault
16             (x => x.Value.Equals(cmbCategories.Text)).Key;
17          reportTemp = projectReport.FindAll(x => x.Category.Equals(key));
18          projectReport = reportTemp;
19      }
20
21      grid.AutoSizeColumnsMode = DataGridViewAutoSizeColumnsMode.None;
22      grid.DataSource = projectReport;
23
24      grid.Columns["Employee"].Visible        = true;
25      grid.Columns["Employee"].FillWeight      = 30;
26      grid.Columns["Project"].Visible          = true;
27      grid.Columns["Project"].FillWeight       = 40;
28      grid.Columns["Manager"].Visible          = true;
29      grid.Columns["Manager"].FillWeight       = 20;
30      grid.Columns["ProjectNo"].Visible        = true;
31      grid.Columns["ProjectNo"].FillWeight     = 20;
32      grid.Columns["ProjectNo"].DefaultCellStyle.Alignment =
33         DataGridViewContentAlignment.MiddleRight;
34      grid.Columns["PSONumber"].Visible        = true;
35      grid.Columns["PSONumber"].DefaultCellStyle.Alignment =
36         DataGridViewContentAlignment.MiddleRight;
37      grid.Columns["PSONumber"].FillWeight     = 15;
38      grid.Columns["Parent"].Visible           = false;
39      grid.Columns["Parent"].FillWeight        = 15;
40      grid.Columns["Hours"].Visible            = true;
41      grid.Columns["Hours"].DefaultCellStyle.Alignment =
42         DataGridViewContentAlignment.MiddleRight;
43      grid.Columns["Hours"].FillWeight         = 15;
44      grid.Columns["ProjectID"].Visible        = false;
45      grid.Columns["ParentID"].Visible         = false;
46      grid.Columns["Department"].Visible       = true;
47      grid.Columns["Department"].FillWeight    = 15;
48      grid.Columns["Category"].Visible         = true;
49      grid.Columns["Category"].FillWeight      = 10;
50      grid.Columns["Grouptag"].Visible         = true;
51      grid.Columns["Grouptag"].FillWeight      = 15;
52
53      Cursor = saveCursor;
54  }
```

Chapter 10

Using Excel

10.1 Exporting Data

When you work within Test & Measurement, you know that no matter how many ways your application can show data, the user will always ask: "can I get it in Excel?" Users want to calculate, filter, sort and sometimes pivot their data in the well-known tool.

There are libraries for exporting, but again I wanted something simple that is easy to maintain, and I did not need advanced coloring etc. - only strings and numbers. It can be difficult to write in the native Excel formats, but CSV - Comma Separated Values - is a simple format that Excel can import.

The most annoying thing - when using CSV - is that you cannot just double-click on a file and sit back while Excel opens it. You are always asked about the formatting. This is tedious if you are opening many files. However, Excel has a well kept "secret". If the first line in the csv-file contains 'sep=;' and nothing else, it will silently accept ';' as column separator and newline[1] as row separator. The code for this is seen in line 18 in Listing 10.1.

---

[1] Actually CR+LF on Windows

Another problem is to get Excel to show unicode characters as those extra
ones in the danish alphabet. The cure for this is found in line 16, where
the *StreamWriter* is asked to use unicode encoding.

Listing 10.1: Export to CSV for Excel

```
 1  private void btnFileSave_Click(object sender, EventArgs e)
 2  {
 3      const string sep = ";";
 4      const string stStr = "=\"";
 5      const string endStr = "\"";
 6
 7      saveReportDlg.AddExtension = true;
 8      saveReportDlg.Filter = "Comma Separated Values "+
 9          "(*.csv)|*.csv|All files (*.*)|*.*";
10      if (saveReportDlg.ShowDialog() == DialogResult.OK)
11      {
12          fileName = saveReportDlg.FileName;
13          try
14          {   // Unicode to support Danish chars!
15              using (System.IO.StreamWriter file = new
16                System.IO.StreamWriter(fileName,false,Encoding.Unicode))
17              {
18                  file.WriteLine("sep=" + sep);
19                  // Write a header
20                  // Project-names go like  ="2250" - with extra "
21                  // around to assure that the 2250 stays text
22                  if (rdBtnTotPerProj.Checked)
23                  {
24                      if (chkMonths.Checked)
25                          exportAmmortizedTotals(
26                              false,file,sep,stStr,endStr);
27                      else
28                      {
29                          file.WriteLine("Grouptag"+sep+"Project"+sep+
30                          "Manager"+sep+"ProjectNo"+sep+"PSONo"+sep+
31                          "Category"+sep+"TopLevel"+sep+"Hours"+sep+
32                          "Closed");
33                          foreach (DBUtil.ProjectReport line
34                            in projectReport)
35                              file.WriteLine(
36                                  stStr+line.Grouptag+endStr+sep+
37                                  stStr+line.Project+endStr+sep+
38                                  stStr+line.Manager+endStr+sep+
39                                  stStr+line.ProjectNo+endStr+sep+
40                                  stStr+line.PSONumber+endStr+sep+
41                                  stStr+line.Category+endStr+sep+
42                                  stStr+((line.ParentID <= 0) ?
43                                      line.Project.ToString() :
44                                      line.Parent.ToString())+endStr+sep+
45                                      line.Hours.ToString()+sep+
46                                  DBUtil.projectsDict[
47                                      line.ProjectID].Closed);
48                      }
49                  }
50  //  Code removed
```

The last little challenge is numbers that are to be interpreted as text. In our case, project names are sometimes numbers, sometimes text. When these get into Excel, the default is that text is left-aligned, whereas numbers are right aligned. This looks terrible. The cure for this is to surround all strings in the endangered columns with a few characters. If e.g. the project name is 123456 we write:

```
="123456"
```

This is done with the help of the two constant strings declared in lines 4-5.

To save space, Listing 10.1 is not complete. The rest is just similar outputs for other reports. The function call in line 25 leads to a related output, that is slightly more complex as it handles *amortized* values - the same data distributed per month. Figure 10.1 shows how such an exported output can be turned into a stacked line-chart in Excel. This is very useful information for management - showing how work is distributed over projects, but also how there may be "seasons" in the total work. The projects are here named P1 to P10 as the legend shows. The stack is the same projects from the bottom. Thus, we have P1 at the bottom and P10 at the top. Normally Excel uses nice different colors - for this illustration patterns are used instead.

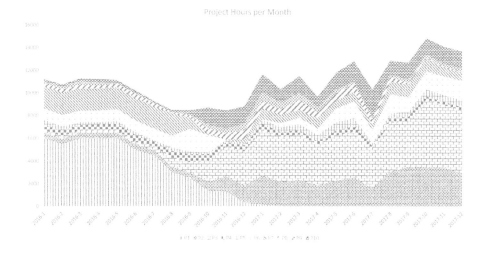

Figure 10.1: Time spent on projects - over time

Returning to Listing 10.1, please note the frequent use of "projectsDict" - the projects dictionary held in the DBUtil layer. This is needed because the SQL behind the project-report only returns the ProjectID - not all the attributes of a project. This is a flexible solution. As more administrators came along, the need for additional columns in the Projects table grew. With a relative low number of projects it makes sense to lookup whatever attributes are needed in a given report, instead of constantly modifying the lower level SQL and the data transfer objects that holds data from it.

10.2   Importing Data

Another common task is importing from Excel. In the TimeReg project an import-dialog was created - allowing selected users to feed a comma-separated file into a DataGridView. If the view looks OK, the data is submitted to the database.

In this case the file is a list of users, with each line looking like e.g.

```
njensen; Niels Jensen; 123456; 6012
```

The fields in the file are the given users netname, full name, salary number and department.

This is an easy way to get departments or divisions on board. Someone in the department generates an Excel sheet with columns as described above, I export to CSV and import into TimeReg.

The code is found in Listing 10.2. Most of the code is input validation - not included here to save space, but can be downloaded. In line 3 we once again define ';' as separator.

In line 14 the "iso-8859-1" encoding is used. This seems to be the preferred encoding used by Excel. It is known as "Latin-1", and is very popular in the western world.

Note that the code allows for two modes: one for inserting new employees, and one for updating existing ones. The latter is mainly to be used in organizational changes where many users move around between departments.

Listing 10.2: Import users from CSV-file

```
1   private void btnFileOpen_Click(object sender, EventArgs e)
2   {
3       char sep = ';';
4       char [] skip = {' ','\t'};
5       int skipcount = 0;
6       int syntaxOKcount = 0;
7
8       ofDlg.AddExtension =true;
9       ofDlg.Filter = "CSV␣(*.csv)|*.csv|Text␣Files␣"+
10          "(*.txt)|*.txt|All␣files␣(*.*)|*.*";
11      if (ofDlg.ShowDialog() == DialogResult.OK)
12      {
13          using (StreamReader sr = new StreamReader(ofDlg.FileName,
14              System.Text.Encoding.GetEncoding("iso-8859-1")))
15          {
16              string line;
17              employees = new List<DBUtil.Employee>();
18
19              while (sr.Peek() >= 0)
20              {
21                  line = sr.ReadLine();
22                  string [] tokens = line.Split(sep);
23
24                  if (tokens.Count() == 4)
25                  {
26  // input and test code skipped
27                      string netname = tokens[0].ToLower();
28  // All four tokens parsed and checked
29  // input and test code skipped
30                      if ((!chkUpdate.Checked && curID == 0) ||
31                          (chkUpdate.Checked && curID != 0))
32                          employees.Add(new DBUtil.Employee(netname,
33                              fullname, number, dept, false, -1));
34                      else
35                          skipcount++;
36                  }
37                  else
38                  {
39                      MessageBox.Show("Using␣separator:␣'"+sep+
40                          "'␣I␣find␣"+ tokens.Count() +"␣tokens␣in:␣"+line,
41                          "Wrong␣no␣of␣tokens␣-␣Expecting␣4");
42                      return;
43                  }
44              }
45          }
46          grid.DataSource = employees;
47          grid.Refresh();
48          chkUpdate.Enabled = false; // Don't allow user to change now!
49
50          MessageBox.Show(skipcount.ToString() + "␣out␣of␣"+
51              syntaxOKcount.ToString()+ "␣ignored", "Status");
52      }
53  }
```

Listing 10.3: Submit Users

```
1  private void btnSubmit_Click(object sender, EventArgs e)
2  {
3      if (!chkUpdate.Checked)
4          foreach (DBUtil.Employee employee in employees)
5              DBUtil.insertNewEmployee(employee);
6      else
7          foreach (DBUtil.Employee employee in employees)
8              DBUtil.updateEmployee(employee);
9
10     // Don't try again
11     btnSubmit.Enabled = false;
12 }
```

Listing 10.3 shows the simple code needed to submit the new or updated users once the super-user has looked at the dialog and accepted it. Since the DataGridView was filled from the "employees" list we use this list directly. Thus, the DataGridView is only written to by the program - never read from.

10.3 Copy-Paste to and from Excel

There are plenty of scenarios where you don't want to import or export whole files from/to Excel. In TimeReg this is relevant when managers create forecasts in the application. They may edit directly in TimeReg - or they might prefer to copy existing data to Excel, edit here and copy back to TimeReg.

The wiring of popup-menu events is shown in Listing 10.4. This ensures that the user via the menu can activate the two functions "pasteCTRLV-ToolStripMenuItem_Click" and "copyCTRLCToolStripMenuItem_Click". The user gets a reminder about the use of CTRL-V and CTRL-C as shortcuts, as the text-strings for these are also shown in the popup-menu.

Listing 10.4: Setting up Events

```
1  deleteToolStripMenuItem.Click      += deleteToolStripMenuItem_Click;
2  pasteCTRLVToolStripMenuItem.Click += pasteCTRLVToolStripMenuItem_Click;
3  pasteCTRLVToolStripMenuItem.ShortcutKeyDisplayString = "Ctrl+V";
4  copyCTRLCToolStripMenuItem.Click   += copyCTRLCToolStripMenuItem_Click;
5  copyCTRLCToolStripMenuItem.ShortcutKeyDisplayString = "Ctrl+C";
```

Interestingly, the two actions - copy and paste - take different routes. If the user presses CTRL-C, there is no action handler for this in our code. Thus, it is the DataGridView's built-in CTRL-C handler that performs the relevant action. If the user activates the menu-item for the same thing, the menu-action simply fakes a CTRL-C, and thus again leaves it to the DataGridView handler. This is seen in Listing 10.5 line 17.

Listing 10.5: Event Handlers

```
1   private void grid_KeyDown(object sender, KeyEventArgs e)
2   {
3       if (e.Control && e.KeyCode == Keys.V)
4       {
5           if (Clipboard.ContainsText())
6           {
7               string oneStr = Clipboard.GetText();
8               pasteText(oneStr);
9           }
10
11          e.Handled = true;
12      }
13  }
14
15  void copyCTRLCToolStripMenuItem_Click(object sender, EventArgs e)
16  {
17      SendKeys.Send("^C");
18  }
19
20  void pasteCTRLVToolStripMenuItem_Click(object sender, EventArgs e)
21  {
22      if (Clipboard.ContainsText())
23      {
24          string oneStr = Clipboard.GetText();
25          pasteText(oneStr);
26      }
27  }
```

For paste, it is the other way around. The CTRL-V keystroke is caught by the code in Listing 10.5 - line 3. The clipboard content is used as parameter into "pasteText". Line 11 assures that the corresponding event-handler in the grid is *not* called. If the corresponding menu-item handler is called (line 20), it too fetches the text in the clipboard buffer and hands it over to pasteText.

Finally, Listing 10.6 shows selected parts of the paste-handler. The text-string from Excel is pretty much like the contents of a CSV-file. Instead of comma-separation it uses tabs to separate rows (like many CSV files).

There are a couple of reasons why CTRL-C can be handled by the Data-

GridView, while the paste requires more code than what fits into a page here:

❐ You cannot mark non-existing cells for copy. In other words, the copy always works on a square of existing cells. This is simple to handle for the standard-code in the DataGridView. A paste however, may be performed on e.g. the bottom line and create a need to add new lines to have something to paste into.

❐ When we copy *from* the application, the DataGridView will supply the visible contents of the cells. If these contain project-names and employee-names (which the leftmost columns do), the text is copied to Excel as is. This is what the user expects. However, when we paste back into the DataGridView, we may need to change the text back into a ProjectID and an EmployeeID. This is because these fields are not usual text-fields, but drop-down boxes that allows managers - per row - to select project and employee. Going further into this will take us too far away from the copy-paste theme in this section.

Listing 10.6: Paste handler

```
1   private void pasteText(string inputStr)
2   {
3   // Where do we start?
4   int row         = grid.CurrentCell.RowIndex;
5   int firstCol     = grid.CurrentCell.ColumnIndex;
6
7   // Columns are split with \t and rows with \r\n
8   string[] rowDelim = new string[] { "\r\n" };
9   string[] colDelim = new string[] { "\t" };
10
11  try
12  {
13  // Split up in lines first
14  string[] lines = inputStr.Split(rowDelim,
15      StringSplitOptions.RemoveEmptyEntries);
16
17
18  foreach (string line in lines)
19  {
20      // Every line starts at the same column as this is a "square-paste"
21      int col = firstCol;
22      // Now split up in columns
23      string[] fields = line.Split(colDelim, StringSplitOptions.None);
24
25  // !!!Skipped code for extending beyond right side or bottom!
26
27              // Now for the actual paste
28              foreach (string field in fields)
29              {
30  // !!!Skipped code for using the string-per-Excel-cell
31                  col++;
32              }
33              row++;
34          }
35      btnSubmit.BackColor = dirty;
36      }
37      catch (InvalidOperationException e)
38      {
39          MessageBox.Show(
40              "Sorry_-_cannot_interpret_data_from_clipboard\r\n"
41              +e.Message, "Illegal_Format");
42      }
43  }
```

Index

In December 2018 Klaus Elk published with De Gruyter, the 3'rd edition of "Embedded Software for the IoT". This is an overview of all the major domains needed when creating embedded products. From CPUs and Operating Systems over Digital Signal Processing and Network Technologies to Encryption and Industry 4.0.

In October 2023 Klaus Elk published "Microcontrollers with C - Cortex-M and Beyond". Klaus Elk demonstrates how Microcontrollers work by debugging samples. We follow the code from compiler, through linker and into the memory. We learn about CMSIS libraries and experiment with FPU and MPU. The book shows parallel patterns and how a Real-Time Operating System works. This is exemplified in the final chapter using FreeRTOS.

www.ingramcontent.com/pod-product-compliance
Lightning Source LLC
LaVergne TN
LVHW081345050326
832903LV00024B/1329